This book is dedicated to my brothers:
Andrew, Gregory, Michael, and Nathan. I love you!

Female Comedic Monologues   Age Range   Page Number

Female Dramatic Monologues   Age Range   Page Number

Either Gender Comedic Monologues

Either Gender Dramatic Monologues

TIPS & TERMS FOR MONOLOGUES AND ACTING

A. **The Basics**:

1. **Text**: All the words you read and speak within the monologue are called the "text".

2. **The Script**: A "script" is a play or screenplay (movie) on paper. A script is what actors use to memorize the text, the lines and sometimes the blocking.

3. **The Lines**: A "line" is a sentence within the text that a character speaks aloud. When an actor says, "I forgot my lines", this means they forgot a few sentences they were to have memorized. This happens to everyone, but the more you rehearse, the better you will remember the lines!

4. **Blocking**: "Blocking" is a term that means the actor was given direction to move to a certain place, at a certain time, and sometimes in a certain way. Sound confusing? It's not so bad! For example: When you see an actor on stage or in a movie walk to the refrigerator, or pick something up, they were told to do that by the director. You can also say "block", as in, "When will we block the scene?" Or, you can say "blocked", as in, "That scene was already blocked".

5. **An Act**: An "Act" is a main section of a play. A play can have one, two, or more Acts, depending on the length of the play. Each time there is a new Act you have a change of place, change of time, or both.

6. **A Scene**: A "Scene" is a distinct section of an Act. Scenes help actors and directors keep the show organized. Movies have scenes, too, but usually not traditional Acts. A change in

place or time are scenes for movies. For example, on DVDs you can choose the option "scene selection" to view specific parts of the movie.

7. **Character**: A "character" is the person, thing, or animal that an actor represents. If you are an actor, then you play the part of someone else, who may be nothing like you, or may be exactly like you!

8. **A Monologue**: A "monologue" occurs when one character is speaking for a minute or more without another character interrupting them. A monologue can tell a whole story, or part of a story. When two characters or more are speaking, this is called **dialogue**.

9. **Memorization**: This happens when you learn something by heart. A beloved college professor gave me the best advice an actor can have on the first day of class. He said, "Memorizing the lines is the easiest part of an actor's job". It's true! Memorizing is easy and takes one afternoon to complete. Children have the unique ability to sponge up information quickly; their ability to memorize lines is quite natural!

10. **Rehearsal**: This is a term that actors use when they practice their material. Whether rehearsing a monologue or a scene, all actors rehearse to make their performance the best it can be. Even though they have similar meanings, rehearsal is not called "practice". Practice is for sports; rehearsal is for acting.

11. **Audition**: This is a term for something like a "job-interview" in the acting world, and THIS is where monologues often come into play. Auditioning your skills as an actor is like a mini-performance for showcasing your ability. If a Casting Director, Producer, Director, or Talent Scout want to see range in an actor's ability, they'll **usually** ask the actor to prepare one comedic and one dramatic monologue, usually one to two minutes in length.

12. **Side:** If an actor is auditioning for something in particular, like a specific character in a play, directors will often provide a **side** from the play or screenplay. A "side" is a section of a script where the character you **read** is speaking. A director may say, "Hello, Taylor. You will be reading for the role of 'Cam' today. Your sides are on the desk just around the corner." You will know that they mean you will read off a paper that has the character Cam's lines when they're speaking in the script.

13. **Audience**: An "audience" is a group of people in front of whom you **perform**.

B. <u>**Cues in the Text for Help with Acting**</u>:

When you understand WHAT you are reading and HOW to read the text, your line **delivery** (the **WAY** you speak the lines) will be much easier for you as an actor. Here are some helpful tips for when you read and memorize your lines:

1. **Periods** and **Commas** in the text are what we call <u>natural pauses</u>. When you see a comma like this , or a period like this . you will pause briefly by taking a breath. This will make the lines you speak more realistic because we take breaths in real-life, naturally!

2. **Ellipses** also mean to pause, but longer than just a breath. This is what ellipses look like ... If you count two breaths this will be a long enough pause where there are ellipses.

3. **Exclamation points** mean that you should sound excited when you read the sentence. This is an exclamation point ! So if you have a sentence that reads, "I ate ice cream with my best friend!", then you should sound excited and happy because of the exclamation point at the end of the sentence.

4. **Question marks**, which look like this **?**   mean that your voice should go up at the end of a sentence. A sentence sounds different if you say, "The pen was in the desk.", rather than, "The pen was in the desk?" Try it out! Speak the sentences out loud.

5. When words are in **CAPITAL LETTERS** you say them with a little more feeling, or emphasis, than usual. BECAUSE WHEN YOU SEE ALL CAPITAL LETTERS IT SEEMS LOUDER THAN WHEN THE LETTERS are lower case. THE SAME GOES FOR SPEAKING THESE WORDS. IF YOU READ ALOUD WHAT YOU SEE HERE, YOU SHOULD BE LOUDER THAN when you read this part of the sentence.

6. If a sentence or word is *italicized* or in CAPITAL LETTERS, and is within a **parenthesis** like this: (*Look the other way*)   Or like this: (PAUSE)   Then the words are **not** to be spoken. They are **stage directions**.

Stage directions are there to help you with the monologue, and you may use them as a guide. They are similar to blocking; you can follow stage directions on the page to help make the delivery easier for you, and they may also help you be more natural with your acting.

7. When you see this in a monologue **(BEAT)**   it means there is a <u>slight pause</u> along with a <u>mood change</u>. If you see this (PAUSE)   there is a <u>slight pause</u>, but not a mood change, unless the stage directions tell you otherwise.

*Special Note! A **beat** is a term created by a famous director named Constantin Stanislavski. Beats helps the actor feel what their character is feeling, and to be more realistic. Actors often find the beats in the text themselves, but to help you along, the beats have been added as suggested stage directions. *

8. Last, but never least, monologues and ANY script you read **are meant to be spoken**. The words are not created for silent reading, they are created for spoken reading, and then monologues and dialogues are to be spoken from memory.

When you look at monologues or plays, try reading them out loud by yourself to see the difference between silent reading, and exploring the text by reading out loud.

C. **Parents and Teachers**:

1. **Suggested Age Ranges**:

A. There are suggested "age ranges" assigned to each monologue. Please keep in mind these are only suggestions. Modifying any monologue to appropriately fit the age of any young actor is highly encouraged. Every age should have the opportunity to broaden their ability through higher standard or more challenging material, and to explore the possibilities of each monologue.

B. For those actors between the ages of 5 and 7, assistance from adults or older helpers is encouraged for learning the lines. One good method for this is to read one line together, and speak it aloud without looking at the script. Then read the next line, and speak aloud the first and second line together. Go onto the third line, etc. **Always use encouragement and positive feedback!**

C. A "**+**" by the number of the suggested age range indicates from that age on up the monologue is appropriate. For example, 8+ insinuates the monologue is intended for ages 8 and up.

2. **Vocabulary:** Each monologue has vocabulary specifically placed for linguistic growth within the suggested age range of the monologue.

3. **Staged Reading**: A staged reading is when an actor or actors perform with the sides or script in-hand. They may have some lines memorized, or no lines memorized at all. There are a few monologues suggested for staged readings, but these may also be attempted for memorized performance. Also, any monologue may be performed as a staged reading.

4. **Cutting** the script is when an actor or director take the initiative to remove a line ("cut" a line or even a single word) to suit the need of the actor, or for time. This may be done as needed. **Adapting** the lines for Special Needs or learning impaired actors is always encouraged.

5. The **approximate length** of each monologue is posted on the page of the monologue. However, the delivery of each monologue by individual actors may fluctuate that indicated time. This is expected to occur, and unless the actor is auditioning, then the time restraint should be ignored.

6. **Sentences beginning with "And"** are to help make the appropriate break in oratorical delivery. If desired, please explain to the students/actors that, under normal circumstances, sentences usually are grammatically incorrect when they begin with the word "and".

If there are any questions about the monologues, how to read them, or understanding the text, feel free to e-mail hollisjean@hotmail.com, and an associate or myself will respond with an answer promptly. Comments are also greatly welcomed. I sincerely wish that you enjoy the material found within this book, and that your child's or student's acting endeavors will be supported by this material. Thank you, and "Break a Leg"!

All monologues are inspired by true events. © 2009 Hollis McLachlan

FISHING WITH GRANDPA
Male   Comedic

••

My pap takes me fishing every summer when we go on vacation. It's fun because he will pack up some sandwiches and sodas to have when we're out in the motorboat. I gather up the fishing tackle and poles, while pap puts some gas in the motor. I like helping with the fishing equipment because I know that grandpa trusts me to get everything in order without having to worry. When pap places the motor on the boat we're off into the lake! He allows me to steer the boat around the lake when we are far enough into the water. Sometimes he lets me steer until we find a good spot to cast our line. When we fish we have to be really quiet because if you talk too loud, the fish will be scared and they wont bite the bait. The bait is usually a worm or a fake fish. I used to need help putting the bait on the hook, but now I can do it by myself. Last year on vacation I caught a 1.5 pound bass with my grandpa. This year, I'm going to try to beat that record and go for a two pounder!

Time: Approximately 1 minute

Age Range: 5 – 8

VOCABULARY:

1. <u>pap</u>- another way of saying grandfather; a nickname for grandpa

2. <u>gather</u>- to bring a bunch of things that are in different places, together in one place. (Like when toys are all over the living room, you can gather them up and put them in a toy box)

3. <u>tackle</u>- the equipment used for a task (like fishing)

4. <u>motor</u>- a machine that makes a boat or other vehicle with an engine move

Notes

BALLET STAR
Female   Comedic

....

I'm a ballerina. I have been in two recitals and one ballet. I was scared to do the ballet because there were a lot of big people in it. The big girls can go up on their very tippy toes and spin really fast! They look so pretty when they do that. Most of them were fairies in the show, but I got to be an angel. There were 10 angels and my spot was number 8, which is my favorite number so that meant good luck. I practiced my dance everyday and had rehearsal 5 times a week for 2 months! There was a lot of rehearsal time, but the big people rehearsed more than the angels did. When we had the show I did a really good job and I wasn't afraid. I think that's because of how much time I spent rehearsing my dance! I got flowers at the end of the show and people clapped for me. Someday I am going to be like the big girls and spin on my tippy toes and wear a tutu! I'm going to rehearse everyday until I'm in high school and THEN maybe I can be a fairy, too. (A happy sigh) I just love being a real-life ballet star!

Time: Approximately 1 minute

Age Rage: 5 – 6

VOCABULARY:

1. <u>ballet</u>- a classical way of dancing with a specific set of rules
2. <u>recital</u>-a performance that shows an artistic accomplishment, like dancing or playing music
3. <u>rehearsal</u>- a special word used in the arts (dance, theatre, singing) to describe practicing
4. <u>tutu</u>- a type of skirt that ballerinas wear

Notes

HOLE IN THE WALL
Male   Dramatic

....

I got a brand-new set of bow and arrows for my birthday. I couldn't wait to try them out! We set up a place outside for me to practice, but I'm not allowed to play with them by myself. Dad or another grown-up has to be with me. One day my friend Josh came over to play. He knew I got a set of bow and arrows and wanted to see them. I didn't think that would hurt anything, so I took them out of their spot and opened them up. Josh picked up a bow and pretended to shoot it, but without the arrows. It looked like fun so I did it, too. We jumped around the living room pretending to be Cowboys and Indians for a while. But then Josh picked up an arrow. Before I had time to say, "put it down", he shot the arrow right into the wall. My mom came running into the room and when she saw the arrow sticking out of the wall she yelled so loud that Josh and I are scared of her forever. Josh had to go home and I got grounded for a week. I really wish my best friend didn't put that hole in the wall. Now I can't play with my bow and arrows until my NEXT birthday.

Time: Approximately 1 minute

Age Range: 5 – 7

VOCABULARY:

1. <u>practice</u>- something you do over and over again so you can become better at it; like playing a sport

2. <u>pretend</u>- to play make-believe

3. <u>grounded</u>- 1. A punishment when a child is in trouble by their parents or guardians; 2. To have privileges taken away

Notes

FRANCES

Female   Comedic

• •

Frances is my imaginary friend. She keeps me company when my friends aren't over, or mommy is too busy to play. I like my imaginary friend. I've had her since I was three years old. She is the same age as me, too. She is really good at reading me books, and making mud cakes, and telling stories about princesses who always have the same name as me! Frances always wears the same purple dress and black shoes. I tell her she needs to get a new wardrobe, but she says "no way" every time. I guess she really likes the purple dresses. Even though Frances wears the same thing all the time, I don't really mind it because it makes her UNIQUE. I like her because she is different, and exciting, and always nice to me. She is the nicest friend I have! We never fight. She always shares and doesn't care if I get to play with the best toys while she plays with all the other ones. Frances may be imaginary, but she is the best friend anyone could ever have!

Time: Approximately 1 minute

Age Range: 5 – 7

VOCABULRY:

1. <u>imaginary</u>- something or someone that is made up; something that is not real

2. <u>wardrobe</u>- all the different types of clothes a person owns

3. <u>unique</u>- something special because it's the only thing like itself

4. <u>share</u>- to allow someone else to play with your toys, food, or spend time with you

Tested by kids!

Notes

_____
_____
_____
_____
_____
_____
_____
_____
_____
_____
_____
_____
_____
_____
_____
_____
_____
_____
_____
_____
_____
_____
_____
_____
_____
_____
_____
_____
_____
_____
_____
_____
_____
_____
_____
_____

GIVE ME MY PUFFY!
Male   Comedic

••

I have a favorite pillow that I've been carrying around with me since I was just a little baby. It's a fluffy blue pillow, and I call it my Puffy. My Puffy goes everywhere with me. He goes to the supermarket, to my friend's house … he'll even go to school with me. And he IS a he, by the way. (PAUSE) He's the most comfy Puffy anyone could have! I can't go to sleep without him, but I can fall asleep the minute he's with me. When I'm sad, one squeeze from my Puffy makes me happy. He's the only person I could ever talk to without feeling silly about what I say. Well, I guess he's not really a person, but you know what I mean. He listens like a champ! When I was a baby, and mommy needed to wash my puffy, I would scream, and scream, and scream until I got him back. But now, I just wait patiently and eat ice cream or do something to pass the time until I get my Puffy back again, nice and warm from the dryer! I'm always going to have my Puffy. Even when I'm a football player in college, my Puffy is going with me! That's what my older brother did with his teddy bear. But shhhh! Don't tell him I told you!

Time: Approximately 1 minute 2 seconds

Age Range: 5 – 6

VOCABULARY:

1. <u>comfy</u>- another way to say comfortable. To feel cozy!

2. <u>college</u>- a school for learning more after high school

3. <u>squeeze</u>- to give a big hug to someone or something

Notes

PRETENDING
Female   Dramatic

....

Sometimes I like to pretend I'm in a fairy tale. I'll go into the woods behind my house and imagine there are little fairies all around me, and they're my friends. The animals are my friends, too. I'll skip around and pretend that I'm looking for my pet doe who is under a magical spell, because she's actually a princess. I take small snacks into the woods with me to eat under the branches of my favorite tree, and sometimes my pet doe will come very close to me! This tree is in the very middle of the woods, and it bends all the way over. It's the best place to play pretend because it can be anything! It can be a secret castle, or a little magical cottage like in "Snow White". I take my friends there when they come to visit, and we like to pretend we're in a far-away land. We climb on the tree and jump from one side to the other, pretending we're on a pirate ship, and we're looking for our missing treasure map where "X" marks the spot! Actually, my friends and I buried a time capsule in the woods, so when we turn 15 we can go to where "X" marks the spot, and dig up the time capsule. There's only one problem. We can't quite remember where "X" is. But that's okay, we planned on using a metal detector to help us anyway. Tomorrow I am going into the woods to nail up a wooden sign I made. The sign has a name on it. My friends and I decided to come up with a name for our woods. It's called "The Magical Gardens". We love going to "The Magical Gardens" to play pretend!

Time: Approximately 1 minute 18 seconds

Age Range: 5 – 8

VOCABULARY:

1. <u>doe</u>- a female deer

2. <u>spell</u>- pretend magic that witches in fairy tales use to turn people into other things like animals, or to make something happen, like snow fall in the summer

3. <u>time capsule</u>- a box or container that you place things in from the present (now) like magazines, a newspaper clipping, and other things that you hide away and don't open for years and years

4. <u>metal detector</u>- a machine used above ground to search for buried metal (like coins) below the ground's surface

Notes

_____

_____

_____

_____

_____

_____

_____

_____

_____

_____

_____

_____

_____

_____

_____

_____

_____

_____

_____

_____

_____

_____

_____

_____

_____

_____

_____

CHEATER-CHEATER
Male   Dramatic

....

My friends like to cheat when we play games. I don't like that because I never cheat and I know it's wrong. If one of my friends is losing, they usually quit right before the end of our game. OR, if we're playing a board game, they will move their pawn further on the board, hoping I don't see them do it. But if I AM losing, I try my best to win until the game is over. And even if I DO lose, it doesn't really matter to me because it is ONLY a game. It could be a video game, a board game, a soccer game; it doesn't matter what, but my friends will cry like babies if they lose. It just seems a bit silly to me to cry over something like losing a game. It's not the end of the world. Games are supposed to be fun! They were INVENTED to be fun, not to make people cry! I guess some of my friends don't understand that yet. I hope they do soon though, because I'm getting tired of playing with cheaters and sore-losers. I want to have fun playing games again!

Time: Approximately 1 minute

Age Range: 5 – 7

VOCABULARY:

1. cheat- sneaky bad behavior that someone does to make it look like they are winning a game, but they are only winning because they broke the rules when they think no one is looking

2. pawn- the piece in a board game that you can pick up and move to show where you are on the board

3. invented- created

4. sore-loser- a person who loses a game and throws a temper tantrum, or gets really upset because they lost

Notes

MY KILLY-KILLY
Female   Comedic

....

When I was a baby I couldn't say kitty-kitty, instead I would say "killy-killy". I LOVED killy-killy's. I thought they were the best invention ever. My mom says I'd get so excited when I saw one that I'd stop breathing and turn red until I'd burst out, "KILLY-KILLY!!!" (BEAT) One day my parents took me to an elderly lady's house who was a friend of theirs. Her name was Olive Snail. She liked sewing things and making blankets, and crafts, and anything pretty for babies to have. Well, when I was at her house, I picked up a pillow that was in the shape of a raccoon, but to me it looked like a kitty cat in trousers. I would NOT put it down for ANYTHING. My parents kept trying to bribe me before we left to put the raccoon back. They'd say, "Haley, honey, if you put the pillow down you'll get a lollipop!" But I held onto my kitty tightly and said, "Killy-Killy, mine!" I didn't know it was a raccoon, but that didn't matter 'cause if it looked like a cat in trousers, then it was a cat in trousers to me. Olive said it was okay if I wanted to keep it because she knew how much I loved kitty-kitty's. So thanks to Olive Snail, I've had my raccoon companion for years. Killy-Killy's name never changed, and to this day I still have him, and plan on keeping him forever. He's had some re-stuffing, and has been patched up with some material and thread, but he's still the cutest Killy-Killy in trousers to me!

Time: Approximately 1 minute 15 seconds

Age: 5 – 7

VOCABULARY:

1. invention- a new item that has been made for the first time; no one else has ever thought of this item before

2. elderly- a person who has become old, like a grandma or grandpa

3. <u>sewing</u>- to sew means you can create things out of cloth with tools called a needle and thread

4. <u>crafts</u>- fun activities you can do to make things

5. <u>trousers</u>- another word for pants

Notes

_____

_____

_____

_____

_____

_____

_____

_____

_____

_____

_____

_____

_____

_____

_____

_____

_____

_____

_____

_____

_____

_____

_____

_____

_____

_____

_____

_____

_____

MY FACE IS STUCK (IN A SMILE)
Male   Comedic

••

(He never stops smiling throughout the monologue.
The actor addresses the audience throughout.)

Some people think I'm just really, really happy. Others guess I must have the best life a person can have. But they're wrong. They're ALLLLLLLL wrong. I have my up and down days like any other person. My life is pretty good, but things can be better. See, the biggest problem I have is that my face is stuck in a smile. STUCK. No matter what I do, no matter how hard I try, I can't stop smiling. You know whose fault this is? My Uncle Joe's. He told me one afternoon before all this smiling business started, that if I told a fib, even the smallest, tiny fib, my face would smile forever until I told the truth. Uncle Joe is a little nuts, so I just let it go. But then my little sister's friend Maggie came up to me last month and asked me if I liked her. *(pause, HUGE smile)* I … ugh … I said "no". *(pause)* It's been 33 days of non-stop smiling since then. I know and YOU know that there is only one way to put an end to all this smiling. Which is why I'm about to walk over to Maggie's lunch table right NOW.

Time: Approximately 1 minute 3 seconds

Age: 6 – 9

VOCABULARY:

1. fib- a white lie

2. business- the way this word is used here is different from what "business" usually means. Here it means "nonsense"

3. stuck- unable to move or get something out of a certain spot

Notes

TOOTH FAIRY, I'M READY!
Female   Comedic

···

Today I lost my first tooth! My friends and cousins already lost their first teeth, and they always get cool stuff from The Tooth Fairy. Christian and Matilda both got five bucks for EACH tooth they've lost. That already makes a combine total of $25, TAX-FREE, exclusively for their piggy banks. My best friend Paige lost her first tooth two months ago, and SHE got a puppy. The Tooth Fairy couldn't fit the puppy under Paige's pillow, so she just stuck it in the kitchen. I feel really bad for my one friend Jamie, though. All she got was a lousy quarter. I told her the reason she got a quarter is probably because her tooth was faulty or defected in some way. That is reasonable to me. I know if I were the Tooth Fairy and came across a defective tooth, I would certainly NOT be happy about it. Oh! But the BEST thing I know about the Tooth Fairy is that my cousin Mariah, who is 14 and knows EVERYTHING, (*Dramatic PAUSE*) actually SAW her. Yeah, uh-huh. SHE – SAW – HER. Mariah told me that she has blue hair and light purple skin, like lilacs, and is as small as her pinky finger! Ha ha! She is so little! I'm going to stay awake and try to see her. But if I can't, that's alright, I'll still have a prize waiting for me in the morning. (PAUSE) I hope it isn't a quarter!

Time: Approximately 1 minute 9 seconds

Age: 5 – 9

VOCABULARY:

1. <u>combine</u>- to bring two or more separate items together

2. <u>exclusively</u>- another way of saying "only"

3. <u>faulty</u>- not perfect, something is out of sorts with the item

4. <u>reasonable</u>- something that is fair and that makes sense

Tested by kids!

Notes

_____
_____
_____
_____
_____
_____
_____
_____
_____
_____
_____
_____
_____
_____
_____
_____
_____
_____
_____
_____
_____
_____
_____
_____
_____
_____
_____
_____
_____
_____
_____
_____
_____
_____
_____

SOMETHIN' SMELLS LIKE BACON
Male   Comedic

••

(This should be read with a "hillbilly" accent, and should be read VERY SLOWLY.)

I lost my pig, yeup. Can't find old Porky anywheres. I says, "Porky! Oh, Porky! Little piggy! Yo daddy Billy is a lookin' fer ya!" But he ain't anywheres, nope. I asked my sister Dorothy if she's seen him. She says, "Billy-Bobby-Boo, what on earth would I be doin' with yo silly piggy?" I looked in the barn, under the shed, in the pond, under my bed, in the laundry room, in the back seat of the car, in the bed of the truuuuuck. But there just ain't nothin' to it. Nope. Porky is missin' and I is never gonna get to play roll-in-the-mud with him again. I guess I could play roll-in-the-mud with Debbie the pig, or Marcy the pig, or Laney the pig … but Porky was my Porky! *(Sniffs the air)* Mmmmmmm! Somethin' smells like bacon! Oh … I hope it ain't Porky!

Time: Approximately 1 minute 10 seconds.

Age: All Ages

VOCABULARY

1. <u>anywheres</u>- this is not how to spell "anywhere", but it is spelled like this here for comedic purposes
2. <u>ain't</u>- a slang word that means "isn't", or "is not"
3. <u>shed</u>- a small building on a person's property that is usually smaller than a garage and is used for storage

Tested by kids!

Notes

DOLL-NATION!
Female   Comedic

....

I love my dolls. I don't care what anyone says, I'll be playing with my dolls until I'm 80-years-old! I have every kind of doll you can think of: An astronaut doll from the 1980's, a shimmer-fun doll from the 90's, a pregnant doll, which my mother gave me when she was going to have my sister. I have a doll in a wheelchair, which is totally cool because there are pretty girls out there in wheelchairs, too. I mean, you name her, and I got that doll. My bedroom looks like the embassy headquarters for the doll world. Seriously, it's like Santa's workshop had an emergency restroom stop and threw up dolls all over my room. (BEAT) Okay, maybe that was a little gross, but it got the point across, right? If there was a Doll-Nation, it should be my room. Which, come to think of it, if there WAS a Doll-Nation, I'd move there. Like, TONIGHT. Oh! Tonight I'm actually going to the second best place on earth! The MALL! (*Aside*) The first best place requires a whole other monologue, involving an oversized mouse walking around on the top of some circular building. You know, they sell dolls from all around the world, there. Dolls from Germany, London, Lithuania, Japan, the list goes on and on. (*End Aside*) Oh … did I mention I'm going to the MALL? They JUST came out with a new Double-Shimmer-Sparkle-Star-Moonlight-Beam Princess Fairy Doll … and I HAVE to have her! I LOVE my dolls!

Time: Approximately 1 minute 10 seconds

Age Range: 5 – 9

VOCABULARY

1. <u>astronaut</u>- a scientist who goes into outer space to work!

2. <u>embassy</u>- the home or offices of an ambassador (which is a person who visits other countries while representing their own country)

3. <u>headquarters</u> – the main meeting place for large, organized groups of people

4. <u>circular</u>- having a shape which is like a circle, but may not be a *perfect* circle

Notes

_____

_____

_____

_____

_____

_____

_____

_____

_____

_____

_____

_____

_____

_____

_____

_____

_____

_____

_____

_____

_____

_____

_____

_____

_____

_____

_____

_____

_____

LISTEN TO THE LIFEGUARD
Male   Dramatic

....

When I went to the beach I wanted to go out real deep in the water. My mom and dad fell asleep on the sand while I was making sandcastles. I saw them napping, and thought it would be okay to take a few steps into the water by myself. I am a big kid, I didn't think I needed them to be with me for a few little steps. So I grabbed my boogie board to sit on, and walked down to the water. The lifeguard saw me and blew his whistle to tell me not to go out too far in the ocean. I put my toes in the water, just like I said I was going to do. But then I just wanted my ankles to go in the water. And then I thought knee-deep wasn't too bad. While the lifeguard wasn't looking, I went JUST up to my tummy, and that was ALL I was going to go. But then the ocean's current suddenly dragged me far out into the deep part. I couldn't stop myself from going out too far and I got really scared. I just held onto my boogie board and yelled for help until the lifeguard brought me back into the main land. I was in a lot of trouble, but my parents were thankful I was safe. I am lucky that nothing REALLY bad happened to me. From now on, I'm going to listen to the lifeguard, and only go out as far as my parents will go with me!

Time: Approximately 1 minute 12 seconds.

Age Range: 5 – 8

VOCABULARY:

1. <u>boogie board</u>- a shorter type of surfboard which you ride on in the ocean by laying across the board on your belly

2. <u>lifeguard</u>- a person at the beach or pool whose job it is to make sure people in the water are safe

3. <u>current</u>- the force that makes the water in the ocean, rivers, and lakes move

Notes

STRANGERS
Female   Dramatic

••

You should never talk to strangers. One time a man walking a puppy came up to me at the park and asked me if I wanted to see some more puppies that were in his car. I was already taught not to talk to strangers so I knew I had to find my babysitter right away. I started walking in the other direction to find her when the man suddenly grabbed my arm. I screamed really loud! He tried to pull me away but I bit his arm. I didn't know what else to do for him to let me go! I ran and kept screaming. Then my babysitter came running after me and picked me up to get away from the stranger faster. He kept running after me until she came to help. When he saw my sitter, his face looked scared, and he ran off to his car. My sitter dialed 9-1-1 on her cell phone and told the police about the man and what his car and puppy looked like. Then the police caught and arrested him. (PAUSE) Even though I didn't talk to the stranger, I was still in a lot of danger. It was very scary but now the bad guy is in jail. The next time my babysitter goes into the bathroom at the park, I'm going in the building with her. I NEVER want that to happen again!

Time: Approximately 1 minute 4 seconds

Age Range: 5 – 7

VOCABULARY:

1. <u>stranger</u>- a person you do not know
2. <u>taught</u>- past and past participle of "teach" – show or explain to someone how to do or understand something
3. <u>arrest</u>- when the police put handcuffs on a criminal and take them to jail

Notes

OVERLOOKED
Male   Comedic

....

(Suggested and highly recommended for Staged Reading)

I'm the second middle child in my family. I have two sisters and three brothers. My oldest sister is the oldest in the group of us kids, and my younger sister is the youngest in the group of kids. There is my older brother who is second born, and then my other older bother who is younger than my oldest brother, but still older than me. THEN there is my youngest brother who is older than my youngest sister, but younger than ME. *(deep sigh)* Try explaining THAT to family friends at every birthday party and picnic imaginable. And I'm always the one getting overlooked, too, because I'm the SECOND middle child. It's bad enough for Ira because he is the first middle child, but try being the SECOND middle child. Plus, I'm not a girl, so my mother doesn't flaunt my achievements every chance she gets like she does with Carol and Anna. I'm not in middle school, so I don't have as much sport activities as my older brothers, therefore dad isn't as excited when it's time to take me to boy-scouts rather than sports. And since I'm not the YOUNGEST boy, I get nothing … NO RECOGNITION. What do I have to do to stop being overlooked? (PAUSE) I think I'll ask pappy to shave my head. THEN I'll stick out and get SOME attention!

Time: Approximately 1 minute 1 second

Age Range: All Ages

VOCABULARY:

1. <u>overlooked</u>- not noticing or ignoring something or someone
2. <u>flaunt</u>- to show off
3. <u>therefore</u>- another way of saying "for that reason"
4. <u>recognition</u>- to show or prove you know that someone or something exists

Notes

ROAD TRIP!
Anyone   Comedic

∙∙

I am SO excited for our family vacation this year! We are going to the beach for two weeks. I love driving to our beach because the car ride is always so much fun. We call the long car ride a road trip. Because it's like a mini vacation itself! We stop for food at awesome places, and refill on gas which, of course, means that we get out of the car for snacks and soda! The only thing I don't really like about the car ride is that it takes 12 hours to get there. It's a REALLY long drive. But I don't mind it too, too much because I get to sleep most of the time. When I'm not sleeping, I play road games with my parents and sister, and whoever else is going along with us. Last year we took Emma's friend, Lacey. Lacey is in the third grade with Emma, so her parents let her go because she is old enough. Plus, she and Emma have been friends ever since they were babies. This year we're taking our cousin Ty with us. He is ten years old and really funny, and should be really good at the road games. (BEAT) But you know what? I feel kinda' bad for one person in particular who goes along with us. That person is daddy because he's the one who has to stay awake to drive the whole ENTIRE time!

Time: Approximately 1 minute 5 seconds

Age Range: 5 – 8

VOCABULARY:

1. <u>vacation</u>- a time of year when a family can all go somewhere to have fun together; a break from everyday life!
2. <u>particular</u>- only ONE thing or person
3. <u>entire</u>- the WHOLE of time or of something

Notes

WHEN I GROW UP, I WANT TO BE LIKE OSCAR

Male   Comedic

....

When I grow up, I want to be just like Oscar. Oscar is 13-years-old, and his hair is all gray. When he brings me a ball it means he wants to play catch. I always know when a visitor is at my house because Oscar will start yapping his head off. Also, when I hear a "thump, thump, thump" at my bedroom door, I know it's Oscar's tail banging against it, waiting for me to come out and play. If you haven't guessed, Oscar is my dog! He is a hound dog. We've been buddies since before I could crawl. And when I grow up, I want to be just like him. He's the perfect companion anyone could ever have. He's a loyal friend, and he listens to you when you're sad, or just want someone to talk to. Plus, I can trust him because he would never tell my secrets to anyone. He's fun to play with, too! We'll race each other, roll around in the mud together, and catch sticks and stuff. He's much better at catching sticks in his mouth than I am, though. So you see, Oscar is a perfect role model. When I'm older, I want to be the best friend a person can have, just like Oscar!

Time: Approximately 1 minute 2 seconds

Age Range: 5 – 7

VOCABULARY:

1. <u>yapping</u>- a high-pitched bark
2. <u>guess</u>- to suppose something but not sure if your idea is correct
3. <u>companion</u>- a great friend
4. <u>loyal</u>- someone who will always be a good friend to you no matter what

Notes

MR. YUCK
Anyone   Dramatic

••

We had a scare today. (PAUSE) My little brother had to be rushed to the hospital. He is only three. I was at my grandparent's house and was washing my hands in the bathroom. Andrew was next to me holding a bottle of yellow allergy pills and shaking it because he liked the noise it made. The cap was on the bottle, of course, so I didn't worry. I left the bathroom but realized I forgot to dry my hands. So I went back in, and saw that Andrew was putting a yellow allergy pill into his nose. I took the bottle and ran into the other room to tell the adults what just happened. "Andrew put a pill up his nose!", I yelled. Mom rushed into the bathroom to grab Andrew. She held his head to try to see the pill. She ended up getting it out, but we had to call 9-1-1 incase some of the medicine got into his blood system. That could have REALLY hurt him because of how little he is. I'm thankful my little brother was alright. But from now on we put Mr. Yuck stickers on medicine and cleaning stuff so Andrew knows not to get into them. And ESPECIALLY not to put anything up his nose!

Time: Approximately 1 minute

Age Range: 5 – 8

VOCABULARY:

1. <u>rushed</u>- to be in a hurry

2. <u>allergy</u>- when a person's body reacts to dust or pollen, or other matter, causing them to sneeze and get runny noses, and many other annoying (and sometimes dangerous) symptoms

3. <u>blood system</u>- all the blood in your body's veins and cells that make it up.

Notes

_____

_____

_____

_____

_____

_____

_____

_____

_____

_____

_____

_____

_____

_____

_____

_____

_____

_____

_____

_____

_____

_____

_____

_____

_____

_____

_____

_____

_____

_____

_____

_____

_____

_____

ALWAYS SAY "NO"
Male   Dramatic

••

Do you know what a stranger is? A stranger is someone you don't know, or don't know very well. Some strangers can be friendly, but some can be dangerous. If a stranger looks a little scary, and they come up to you and ask if you want candy, run the other way. You should yell, "Fire!", when you're running because then people will pay serious attention to you. You know why? Because a lot of kids yell "help" when they're just playing with each other on the playground, or in a backyard. So if you yell "Fire!", you can get attention quicker. Sometimes strangers AREN'T scary looking, though. They can LOOK really nice, and BE really friendly. But even if those kind of strangers try to give you candy, or ask you to leave with them, or want you to do something you don't want to do, DO NOT DO IT! Don't take the candy, don't go anywhere with them, and DON'T do anything you don't want to do. Run for help. You might never see your family again, or worse. I don't want to think of anything worse than not seeing my family again, but it can happen. So be careful, and always say "no" to strangers.

Time: Approximately 1 minute 10 seconds

Age Range: 5 – 7

VOCABULARY:

1. <u>dangerous</u>- something that CAN hurt you if you are not careful

2. <u>serious</u>- here, serious means the people who hear you yell, will consider your yelling to be something important and not just playing

3. <u>quicker</u>- faster than usual

Notes

_____
_____
_____
_____
_____
_____
_____
_____
_____
_____
_____
_____
_____
_____
_____
_____
_____
_____
_____
_____
_____
_____
_____
_____
_____
_____
_____
_____
_____
_____
_____
_____
_____
_____
_____
_____

LOST
Anyone   Dramatic

I got lost at the mall once when I was with my grandma. She had to look for some clothes for a present, and I had to stay right by her. It was so BORING. I really wanted to go to the toy store, but I wasn't allowed until grandma bought her presents. Since I was bored, I decided to hide in the clothes racks. I like to do that for fun in department stores. But when I came out from hiding in the clothes after a little while, I couldn't find my grandma. I looked all over the department, but she was nowhere in sight. I was getting worried and started to cry. A lady with a nametag came up to me and asked what was wrong. I told her I lost my grandma in the store and didn't know what to do. She took me by the hand and we went into an office where the lady gave me a lolly-pop and made a few phone calls. After about 10 minutes my grandma showed up with her bag of clothes and took me out of the office. We didn't go to the toy store that day because I didn't listen to her. I walked away without telling grandma where I was going. The next time I go anywhere with an adult, I'm going to stay right by them so I don't get separated from their side. (BEAT) And also so I can go to the toy store!

Time: Approximately 1 minute

Age Range: 6 – 7

VOCABULARY:

1. lost- to lose your way, to become separated from the people you're with, and not know where they are

2. boring- to feel dull, not excited or happy at ALL

3. department- section of a store that is designated for certain items

Notes

_____
_____
_____
_____
_____
_____
_____
_____
_____
_____
_____
_____
_____
_____
_____
_____
_____
_____
_____
_____
_____
_____
_____
_____
_____
_____
_____
_____
_____
_____
_____
_____
_____

I HATE MYSELF
Male   Dramatic

....

(Based on real people and actual events.)

I HATE myself. Everything always goes wrong because of me. My sissy doesn't love me because I am bad to her. My brother doesn't love me because I always try to beat him up, and mommy gets really mad at me when I break her things. But I can't HELP it! I know I sometimes have bad behavior, but it is because my batteries aren't working right. I have something called Asperger's Syndrome. That is like autism, and you sometimes can't help it to have bad behavior. Sometimes I need to tell my brain really hard to listen and be good. But sometimes I don't WANT to be good because it makes my belly hurt, and I need to throw up. Mommy says we don't go anywhere because people look at me funny and are mean to me, and say mean things to mommy like, "Can't you control your own child?" I don't know what they mean, but it doesn't sound very nice. Mommy says just because I look normal, other people think they can be rude when I have bad behavior. They think that if I look like a regular kid, I should act like a regular kid. And I TRY, but sometimes I can't get my batteries to work right. But no one likes me when I'm nice or try to be nice ANYWAY. No one understands. The doctors don't understand! I DON'T EVEN UNDERSTAND! I hate this feeling so much.

Time: Approximately 1 minute 25 seconds

Age Range: 7 – 9

VOCABULARY:

1. <u>batteries</u>- containers that convert energy into power to make electronic devices work

2. <u>autism</u>- neurological disorder that affects a person's ability to communicate, their social interactions, and responses to their environment

3. <u>regular</u>- a way to describe something that an entire society accepts

4. <u>Asperger's Syndrome-</u> a syndrome that lays on the autism spectrum, where a person might be able to speak "normally", but still have trouble with social interaction and other communications

Notes

_____

_____

_____

_____

_____

_____

_____

_____

_____

_____

_____

_____

_____

_____

_____

_____

_____

_____

_____

_____

_____

_____

_____

_____

_____

_____

_____

_____

_____

FAVORITES
Female   Dramatic

....

I asked my mom last night who her favorite was between me and my two sisters. She said she didn't have a favorite and that she loves all of us the same. I said that grandma has a favorite and that it is Olivia. Olivia gets ALL of grandma's attention and since she is the littlest, grandma will always love HER best. Mommy said it wasn't true and that grandma isn't allowed to have a favorite because all of us girls are special in every way, and not just Olivia. But I said Olivia always gets read whatever story she wants, and as many TIMES as she wants it. Sometimes I don't even get to have a story read to me. When we go to the movies with grandma, Olivia picks out what we will watch, and she gets the MOST popcorn. Mom says grandma shouldn't do those things and that me and Jenny are just as wonderful and important as Olivia. But that doesn't change grandma's liking Olivia the best. (PAUSE) Sometimes I wish I was someone's favorite little girl. Even if it isn't grandma's, it'd be fun to be a favorite.

Time: Approximately 1 minute

Age Range: 5 – 7

VOCABULARY:

1. <u>favorite</u>- a thing or person you like more than anything else
2. <u>attention</u>- special notice of something or someone
3. <u>important</u>- to have a huge amount of value or worth

Notes

JORDAN NEEDS TO LEARN
Male   Dramatic

••

I like going to my friend Jordan's house. We play video games, and eat junk food, and watch super-hero movies. But Jordon needs to learn to be good behavior. He can be really, REALLY bad sometimes. He likes to cheat at the games we play, and sometimes he says, "Shut up". If I said, "shut up" in front of MY parents, I'd get soap shoved into in my mouth! But his parents just say, "Oh Jordan, stop that." I really thought he would learn to be good when Christmas came last year. I thought Santa would put coal in his stocking for being bad, and then he would KNOW to stop the bad behavior. But Santa found it in his dear heart to give Jordan ALL the presents he asked for. Talk about generosity. I couldn't believe it. Santa was really nice for doing that, but it didn't help Jordan to behave any better. (PAUSE) Jordan needs to learn to be good behavior and not cheat at our games or say mean things to me. If he doesn't stop it, I don't think I can be his friend much longer!

Time: Approximately 1 minute 1 second

Age Range: 5 – 7

VOCABULARY:

1. behavior- the way you act; for example, if you are being good, then you are demonstrating good behavior!

2. shoved- to push someone or something really hard

3. generosity- to be giving toward others, simply out of the kindness of your heart

Notes

DADDY'S DEPLOYED
Male   Dramatic

··

My dad is in the military. He works really hard everyday and every night to keep my family and friends safe. The only part I don't like is not seeing him. He was deployed to another country three months ago. He calls mommy and me on the phone to tell us all his exciting stories about what he sees that is different in other places that our home doesn't have. He tells us about all the work he does and how much he likes it, but he also misses us "too much." I tell him that all the time. I really, really, really miss him. He says that he is proud to keep our country safe. I try hard to understand that daddy is being a hero, but I still wish he was here with me and mommy and the new baby. My baby sister Natalie will be over a year old before she sees daddy for the first time. I show her pictures and videotapes of daddy, so those help. I asked mommy if we could all get in a plane and go visit daddy. She said we weren't allowed because part of the job of being a hero means making sacrifices, including being in places too dangerous for families to visit. (PAUSE) Even if daddy wasn't in another country, he would still be me and Natalie's hero. I can't wait for him to be home again.

Time: Approximately 1 minutes 6 seconds

Age Range: 6 – 8

VOCABULARY:

1. <u>military</u>- the armed forces of a country
2. <u>deployed</u>- to be moved to another country or place
3. <u>sacrifice</u>- to give something (you love) up for a while for a very good reason

Notes

_____
_____
_____
_____
_____
_____
_____
_____
_____
_____
_____
_____
_____
_____
_____
_____
_____
_____
_____
_____
_____
_____
_____
_____
_____
_____
_____
_____
_____
_____
_____
_____
_____
_____
_____
_____
_____

DENIED
Male   Dramatic

....

I'm never allowed to do anything I want to do. I ask my mom for ice cream after dinner, she yells, "No! You didn't finish your carrots!" But she'll give ice cream to my brothers. I ask dad if I can go fishing with him and his friends. He says, "No. You're too little. I'll take you some other time, just you and me." But we haven't gone fishing yet. I ask my brothers if I can build blocks with them, or play a game, or ANYTHING. But they just yell, "NO!", and slam the door in my face. At least mom and dad explain themselves when they say no. But still, I'd actually like to do something I want to do, or HAVE something I'd like to have for a change. I'm tired of everyone always telling me no. I'm a person too! I might be little, I might be somewhat misbehaved sometimes, but THAT doesn't mean that I don't deserve something I like once in a while! What about MY feelings? Don't I have rights? It's always no, no, no. Well, I say it's time to loosen up you pride. I mean, give a boy a bowl of ice cream for goodness sake, even if he DOESN'T finish all of his carrots. What's the harm in that?! I've heard that there are actually two stomachs: ONE for dinner, and ONE for desert!

Time: Approximately 1 minutes 15 seconds

Age Range: 5 – 8

VOCABULARY:

1. <u>explain</u>- to describe something by using details

2. <u>somewhat</u>- another way of saying "a little bit"

3. <u>deserve</u>- to earn something (rewards OR punishments) for a person's behavior

4. <u>pride</u>- a feeling a person has which is usually that they are the best at everything and right about everything

Notes

_____
_____
_____
_____
_____
_____
_____
_____
_____
_____
_____
_____
_____
_____
_____
_____
_____
_____
_____
_____
_____
_____
_____
_____
_____
_____
_____
_____
_____
_____
_____
_____
_____
_____
_____
_____

PIE HEAD
Anyone   Comedic

··

When I was a baby, my face was really round. I'm talking, I had one HUGE head! Mom thought my big, but adorable head was funny, so she nick-named me Pie Head. Since my face was perfectly round like a pie, the nick-name stuck. But then my head kept getting rounder, and bigger! In the pictures I have of me between the ages of one and three, my head almost takes up the whole paper! I look like a bobble-head toy. Grandma tells me that she and mommy started to worry that my head would never stop growing. They were afraid that I wouldn't fit through doorways or into my first base-ball cap. She said I had a hard time standing up and was a late-bloomer walking because my head weighed too much. But then one day when I was three, my head finally stopped growing and my body caught up with it. From that point on everything grew normally. My family still calls me Pie Head, even though my head isn't NEARLY as huge or round as it once was. Bt it is still PERFECT like it always has been … it just doesn't look so big now!

Time: Approximately 1 minute 2 seconds

Age Range: 6 – 9

VOCABULARY:

1. <u>huge</u>- something that is very, very big

2. <u>adorable</u>- someone or something that is charming, lovable, and attractive

3. <u>nick-name</u>- a name someone is called by friends or family, but is not their ACTUAL name

4. <u>perfect</u>- when someone or something has no faults or errors; excellent in every single way (but don't worry, NO ONE on earth is perfect!)

Notes

DON'T SUCK YOUR THUMB
Male   Dramatic

••

Tommy sucks his thumb. Since he is my age, he should stop or else he'll get bucked teeth. His two front teeth are already starting to stick out a little bit. My teacher tells him over and over again to stop sucking his thumb, because he's too old for that. But he just keeps doing it. His mom is the librarian at our school, and she is *really* mean, especially to Tommy. I told my mom about it and she just rolled her eyes and said his parents are probably "perfectionists". I don't know what she means, but I'm sure it isn't good. Mom is a psychologist, and I hear her telling daddy that some of the kids my age she talks with have parents that try to make them perfect ... she calls them "neurotic perfectionists who give their children neurotic neurosis". But she also says that most of time the kid is just stuck in a bad-habit. (BEAT) I hope Tommy quits his bad habit soon because he will be made fun of, or worse, for having bucked teeth. I'm just glad my parents aren't perfectionists!

Time: Approximately 1 minute

Age Range: 6 – 9

VOCABULARY:

1. <u>bucked teeth</u>- when someone's two front teeth poke up and outward

2. <u>perfectionist</u>- someone who is obsessed with having everything be perfect all the time ... which is unrealistic

3. <u>psychologist</u>- a doctor who helps people understand why they do certain things or think in a certain way

4. <u>neurosis</u>- mild mental illness that involves symptoms of stress

Notes

MOMMY HAS CANCER
Female   Dramatic

I worry about my mommy a lot. She is really sick and has to stay overnight in the hospital all the time. She has not been home in 4 weeks and I get more and more worried about her everyday. I pray for her when I wake up, and I pray on the bus … whenever I get a chance, I'll pray for mommy to get better. But she has not come home yet. When I visit her in the hospital, she seems to be okay. But right when it is time for me to go, mommy always looks pale and like she's going to faint if she doesn't shut her eyes. Her doctor says she has something called cancer. They need to give mommy a special kind of surgery to help her, but I hear daddy say on the phone that it doesn't mean mommy will get better. I hope mommy gets better soon because I miss her. I hope the doctors can fix her up when they do the special surgery. Mommy said that as long as I don't give up hope for her, she'll keep fighting for me. I told her it was a deal because that is one thing I'll always have. I'll always have hope for my mommy. (BEAT) She'll be better soon. The surgery will help her, she'll come home, and daddy and me and mommy will be all happy again.

Time: approximately 1 minute 8 seconds

Age Range: 6 – 8

VOCABULARY:

1. <u>worry</u>- when you feel upset and keep thinking about something that bothers you
2. <u>hospital</u>- a building where doctors and nurses work, and that patients can stay for a long period of time
3. <u>faint</u>- when someone suddenly loses consciousness
4. <u>cancer</u>- a disease caused by an uncontrolled cluster of abnormal cells in a person's (or animal's) body

Notes

A SMALL DISASTER
Male   Comedic

··

My sister Hollie is 15 years older than me, and she just got married last week. I can't understand WHY Liam wanted to marry her, but I HOPE he's happy. The wedding took forever. I had to wear a suit that was about two times too big for me, and carry this silly pillow with the rings on it. After the ceremony, we had to go get pictures taken. This was where the disaster happened. I'll occasionally play teeny, tiny jokes on Hollie, but this was a total accident. See, I made dad pull in a drive-through so I could get some pancakes with syrup, because I was STARVING and couldn't wait for the reception. Well, while the photographer was setting up on the golf course, and I was chowing down on my pancakes, Hollie came over to give me a big, sloppy kiss ... right as I was taking a bite. So naturally, I leaned back to avoid her. As I was pulling away, Hollie lost her balance and fell straight into the plate and got syrup all over the front of her wedding dress. (PAUSE) I wish I would have just let the goof-ball kiss me. At first, there was nothing but chaos. Mom was yelling at me, and crying over Hollie. Dad and Liam were laughing, but dad still made me sit in the back of the van until Hollie was cleaned up and ready for photos. Needless to say, THOSE pancakes were thrown away ... such a total waste. I was grounded for a week, too. The thing I don't understand is, after all the syrup was cleaned up and we got to the reception, Liam smashed cake right into Hollie's face anyway, and even got some on her dress. She didn't cry or yell at HIM!

Time: Approximately 1 minute 30 seconds

Age Range: 6 – 10

VOCABULARY:

1. <u>ceremony</u>- a celebration that takes place with a few expected rules

2. <u>disaster</u>- a sudden accident that causes a lot of damage

3. <u>starving</u>- when a person or animal goes for days without eating; here, starving is used to exaggerate how hungry the character feels

4. <u>chaos</u>- a total mess of things; too much disorder

Notes

_____

_____

_____

_____

_____

_____

_____

_____

_____

_____

_____

_____

_____

_____

_____

_____

_____

_____

_____

_____

_____

_____

_____

_____

_____

_____

_____

_____

_____

TEASING ISN'T NICE
Female   Dramatic

••

Today I went to day camp with a bunch of girls from my neighborhood. Camp is supposed to be fun. There are a lot of crafts and activities to do there. But I haven't been having such a great time. Two blonde girls were teasing me about my clothes today. They said, "Hey, Sandy. You look SO pretty in that skirt." I thought they were being nice so I said, "Oh. Thank you." But then they both looked at each other and said, "Yeah, right!" Then they laughed and walked away. I could hear them talking about me and calling me "nerd" and "loser". (BEAT) I was never mean to them, or said anything nasty about them to their face OR behind their backs. I'm not that type of person. But when I told one of the counselors about what the girls said, all she told me was that I needed to stick up for myself and not let it bother me. (PAUSE) But it DOES bother me. Why are people mean just to be mean? I really don't like people who act that way. Those girls need to learn a lesson in being nicer to others, who never did anything to them at all.

Time: Approximately 1 minute 2 seconds

Age Range: 7 – 10

VOCABULARY:

1. <u>teasing</u>- to make fun of someone with the intention of hurting their feelings
2. <u>counselor</u>- here, this word means a person who supervises children at a camp
3. <u>lesson</u>- something that is to be learned

Notes

_____
_____
_____
_____
_____
_____
_____
_____
_____
_____
_____
_____
_____
_____
_____
_____
_____
_____
_____
_____
_____
_____
_____
_____
_____
_____
_____
_____
_____
_____
_____
_____
_____

MOTHER'S DAY WITHOUT MOM
Male   Dramatic

Today I made my mommy a beautiful present. It's a card with paper flowers for Mother's Day. If I post it now, she might get it on time. I can't see her this Mother's Day because she's far away. (PAUSE) I miss her a whole lot. She's been gone since last September. Daddy said we'll see her again soon ... but it's been so long now. I'll get presents and cards with money in them from her every now and then ... but it isn't the same. I miss SEEING her face, and hearing her voice. Daddy says that where mommy is there aren't any telephones. I asked if we could go visit. Daddy said it's too scary for me . (BEAT) How could the place where mommy is be scary? (PAUSE) I remember the last time I saw her. She looked really sad and was crying a little bit. She told me she was sorry, but I don't know for what. I asked her, "Mommy, why are you sorry?" But she didn't answer, she just hugged me and walked away. I wish I knew where she is and what she's doing. But for now all I can do is mail her my present and hope it gets to her in time for Mother's Day. (PAUSE) I really miss her a lot.

Time: Approximately I minute 5 seconds

Age Range: 6+

VOCABULARY:

1. receive- to get something that was given by someone else

2. mail- letters and packages that are sent and received

3. post- another way of saying "to mail"

Notes

_____

_____

_____

_____

_____

_____

_____

_____

_____

_____

_____

_____

_____

_____

_____

_____

_____

_____

_____

_____

_____

_____

_____

_____

_____

_____

_____

_____

_____

_____

_____

_____

WHERE IS BOO-BOO?
Female   Dramatic

....

When I came home from school one day, I went to feed my bird Boo-Boo like I always do. Boo-Boo was a yellow canary, and he sang the most beautiful songs. He was so cute and made me very happy. (BEAT) But when I went to go feed him, Boo-Boo wasn't in his cage. I couldn't figure out how he got out so I called for him, "Boo-Boo! Boo-Boo! Where are you?" Then my mom walked into the living room and told me the worst news I ever heard. She said that Boo-Boo was very old, and when living creatures get old they die and go to Heaven. (PAUSE) I cried for a really long time but mom said, "Don't worry. You were a good mommy to Boo-Boo and he'll always be with us, even though we can't see him." (PAUSE) We buried Boo-Boo in the back yard right by the yellow flowers to remind us of him. Even though he isn't alive anymore I know he is with me and still loves me and my family, just as much as we love him. (PAUSE) We have a new birdie now. And she's pretty and sings beautiful songs, too. But we'll never forget about Boo-Boo.

Time: Approximately 1 minute 2 seconds

Age Range: 5 – 7

VOCABULARY:

1. <u>canary</u>- a small yellow bird
2. <u>creature</u>- an animal
3. <u>forget</u>- to not remember something that you once knew

Notes

A SCARY PLACE TO LIVE
Male   Dramatic

••

My family always overlook me. They aren't very nice to me, either. They LOVE my two older brothers ... but not me. At Christmas, my brothers always get more presents than I do. My mom will make me clean the house and she'll hit me when she thinks I don't clean good enough. While I clean, my brothers get to watch T.V. (PAUSE) Can someone please EXPLAIN this to me? Why am I always getting the short end of the stick? That's what my grandparents say to me. They're the ONLY nice people in my family, and the ONLY people who love me. They say the way my dad lets my mom yell at me and make a slave out of me is unbelievable. They tell me all the time that they want me to live with them so I can be happy. They said they will treat me like a regular boy and not a servant. (PAUSE) Sometimes I wish that I COULD just fly over to where they are and hide where I'll be safe. But no one gets how bad it is with my mom. Everyone ... the teachers, the doctors ... they think I'll be just fine. (PAUSE) All I can say is I hope so.

Time: Approximately 1 minute 3 seconds

Age Range: 7+

VOCABULARY:

1. <u>overlook</u>- to ignore someone or something, sometimes on purpose, sometimes by accident

2. <u>slave</u>- a person who is forced to work without getting paid

3. <u>unbelievable</u>- a fact that is difficult to believe

Notes

_____
_____
_____
_____
_____
_____
_____
_____
_____
_____
_____
_____
_____
_____
_____
_____
_____
_____
_____
_____
_____
_____
_____
_____
_____
_____
_____
_____
_____
_____
_____
_____
_____
_____
_____

MOM'S A SUPERSTAR
Female   Comedic

••

My mom is the best mom a girl could have. She's a Super Star! She wakes up extra early to make sure I eat breakfast and go to school on time. Sometimes, on her way to work, she'll drive me to school and when I wave good-bye I swear her eyes sparkle. She's so beautiful! Plus, mommy is a super good person. Her job is to make sure animals stay healthy. Yeup! She's a vet! She takes care of dogs, and cats, and birds … any animal you can think of! On the weekend she goes to the zoo in the afternoons to check up on the tigers. I like to go to the zoo with her and learn about all the animals. I want to be a vet like my mommy someday. But this isn't all. At night my mom comes home and makes us dinner before she even has a chance to sit down. Mommy never complains about anything and always has something nice to say about someone. Even bank robbers. Once on the news we saw a bank robber who was caught by the police. Mommy just shook her head and said, "The poor guy HAS to have something wrong with him if he feels the need to rob a bank. Healthy thinking people wouldn't do such a thing". (PAUSE) I don't know where she comes up with this stuff. But she's so sweet, and kind, and loving to everyone and everything, and that to me makes her the biggest superstar in the whole universe. You don't have to be famous to be a superstar. You just have to be a good person … like my marvelous mom!

Time: Approximately 1 minute 19 seconds

Age Range: 7 – 11

VOCABULARY:

1. sparkle- to shine really bright, and twinkle

2. vet- short for veterinarian, which is an animal doctor

3. universe- another way of saying outer space

Notes

_____

_____

_____

_____

_____

_____

_____

_____

_____

_____

_____

_____

_____

_____

_____

_____

_____

_____

_____

_____

_____

_____

_____

_____

_____

_____

_____

_____

_____

_____

_____

WHEN FRIENDS MOVE AWAY
Anyone   Dramatic

••

My friend Pat just moved away this weekend. I don't know what to do right now, because Pat and I used to do EVERYTHING together. Riding my bike without Pat will be boring; playing in the woods without Pat will be useless; I can't play a game of red-light, green-light by myself … there's just nothing to do now! Pat was my best friend, and now (he/she) is in the middle of Utah. I can't ride my bike to the middle of Utah! My parents would verbally slaughter me. Plus it'll take forever. I'm going to be lonely at lunch now, too. No one else is as funny as Pat, or understands me like (he/she) does. Pat and my parents said we can write and visit each other over summer vacation … but what about right NOW? What do they expect me to do in the meantime? My mom says that I'll make a new best friend soon. She says it's not that I'll forget about Pat, I'll just replace (him/her) for a little bit. (PAUSE) REPLACE?! How does she think I'm going to be able to "replace" my number one best-best-BESTEST friend? (PAUSE) I think my other friends are fun and cool, and everything … but no one can ever replace Pat. Ever.

Time: Approximately 1 minute 3 seconds

Age Range: 6 – 11

VOCABULARY:

1. <u>Utah</u>- one of the 50 states in the United States of America

2. <u>verbal</u>- relating to words

3. <u>slaughter</u>- to kill animals for food (in a humane way)

4. <u>replace</u>- when something takes the place of something else

Notes

PEANUT THE ACORN
Female   Comedic

··

(Staged Reading recommended for ages 5 and 6)

Hi. My name is Peanut. No one ever gets that. Other nuts often ask me, "Why is an acorn named Peanut? What FAMILY of ACORNS has the nerve to name their daughter PEANUT?" The answer to that question is MY family. Mom always gets defensive about it. She'll say, "Peanut is a perfectly good name for a beautiful young acorn." This is coming from a grown acorn named Oak. I guess silly names just run in the family. But there is a rational explanation for MY name. The actual reason my name is Peanut is because, like my brother Walnut, I'm adopted. Walnut really is a walnut. But when my mom and dad adopted me form the Adopt-A-Nut agency, they thought I was a misshaped peanut. When I got a little bigger they started to realize that I wasn't a peanut at all. I'm actually an acorn just like them. Walnut makes fun of me and says that the reason everyone thought I looked like a peanut was because I fell too far form the acorn tree. I know he's just kidding. Many baby nuts look alike at first. Like mommy Oak says, "We all start out from similar-looking seeds anyway!"

Time: Approximately 1 minute

Age Range: 5 – 9

VOCABULARY:

1. <u>similar</u>- two or more things that are a like

2. <u>nerve</u>- here, the word refers to someone taking a risk

3. <u>rational</u>- to think and act clearly; with common sense

Notes

ROCKET-POCKET-SOCKET MAN
Male   Comedic

I am the greatest super-hero the world has ever known! I fly at the speed of lighting and can lift buildings off the ground in a matter of seconds! (*Looks at the audience*) My name, you ask? What could it BE you say? (*With confidence*) Tell me, WHO is there to catch your car when you've gone over a cliff? Me! Who cooks your dinner when you've burnt the chicken? Me! What's my name?! It's ROCKET-POCKET-SOCKET MAN! R.P.S. for short. Call information if you need to reach me in an emergency. But I can guarantee that won't be necessary. I have a built-in pocket-socket radar which informs me of trouble 3 minutes before it happens. Since my rocket power helps me fly at the speed of light, it's easy to get to the source of trouble in a jiffy, and pocket the problem away. Which is why my name is ROCKET-POCKET-SOCKET MAN! I'll be available for autographs and commentary after the show. But first! I am off to save an old lady who is about to walk into a ditch. Give me 2.5 minutes. (*Runs out of room, calling*) I'll be right back!

Time: Approximately 1 minute 2 seconds

Age Range: 7 – 10

VOCABULARY:

1. <u>confidence</u>- to be sure of yourself; you believe you can do something no matter what

2. <u>snatches</u>- to grab something very quickly

3. <u>information</u>- here, this means to dial the operator on a telephone

4. 4, <u>commentary</u>- to speak about something specific to a large group of people

Notes

YOU'RE NOT LEAVING!
Female   Comedic

••

Look, mom. I know you think you're going out tonight ... but it's not happening. (PAUSE) No, you're not leaving. There is too much you still need to do tonight, and I'm afraid when you're finished it'll be bed time. (PAUSE) Well, for one, you STILL have to play the board game with me that I very carefully set up for us. (BEAT) No, tomorrow is not good for me. I still have two pages left to color in the coloring book grandma bought me for my birthday, and I was planning on wrapping that up tomorrow. (BEAT) WAIT! Don't go out the door! Ugh ... okay, okay so maybe I can fit the board game somewhere in my schedule for tomorrow. But you can't forget about the laundry that needs done, mom. I mean, that IS your responsibility you know. (PAUSE) Oh no, no, you see ... you THINK you did it all today, but I'd check again if I were you. (BEAT) Grounded? ME?! But mom, I'm your little princess, and princesses don't get grounded. (BEAT, *face changes expression*) Of course I want you to have fun every now and then, but I don't want you to leave right now. (BEAT) WHO is babysitting me? (*big smile*) Angela Doekey?! Well you go ahead and have a great time tonight, mom, and don't worry about the laundry, I was only kidding! You deserve a little break anyway.

Time: Approximately 1 minute 8 seconds

Age Range: 7 – 10

VOCABULARY:

1. <u>wrapping</u>- here, wrapping means to completely finish something.

2. <u>schedule</u>- someone's plans on a day-to-day basis

3. <u>responsibility</u>- when a person has something in particular that they must do and are expected to do

Tested by kids!

Notes

_____
_____
_____
_____
_____
_____
_____
_____
_____
_____
_____
_____
_____
_____
_____
_____
_____
_____
_____
_____
_____
_____
_____
_____
_____
_____
_____
_____
_____
_____
_____
_____
_____
_____
_____

I AM A PRINCESS!
Female   Comedic

···

Nicole, you aren't getting it. When I say I am a princess I don't mean "mommy's little princess" or "princess of my house", or even "princess of the world!" What I mean is simply that I AM a princess. (BEAT) No, no, no! You got it all confused. (*Take a deep , over-exaggerated breath*) Alright, I'll start from the beginning. Once in a land far-far away called Switzerland, there were princes and princesses. There were also a few kings and queens around, too. Anyway, my great-great-great-great a thousand greats grandma was one of those princesses. Her daddy played the clarinet in the Royal Court orchestra and one day she met a dashing prince who married her. Then one of the queens said the poor people should eat cake. Everyone in Christendom got mad at her for saying that, although personally, I'd rather eat cake than green beans. Well, they were mad and said, "Off with her head!" And then there was a big war with fighting cards, and Alice woke up. (PAUSE) Wait … sorry, wrong story. There was a big war with fighting soldiers and they chopped the evil queen's head off. My great-great-great-great a thousand greats grandmother decided that she should book-it so she wouldn't get run over by a solider, or worse, a soldier's horse. So she and the prince ran away from the Russian army, and they settled here. So I really AM a princess, but the 1970s was a *really* long time ago, which makes it nearly impossible to prove. But there's always DNQ testing!

Time: Approximately 1 minute 18 seconds

Age Range: 8 – 10

VOCABULARY:

1. <u>confused</u>- not able to understand something, or not able to think clearly

2. <u>orchestra</u>- a group of musicians who play instrumental music
3. <u>impossible</u>- not able to exist or happen

Notes

_____

_____

_____

_____

_____

_____

_____

_____

_____

_____

_____

_____

_____

_____

_____

_____

_____

_____

_____

_____

_____

_____

_____

_____

_____

_____

_____

_____

_____

_____

_____

_____

DON'T PLAY WITH MATCHES
Male   Dramatic

....

I used to think matches were the coolest things ever. When I would stay the night at my friend Christopher's place, we would wait for his mom to fall asleep so we could grab the matches from their secret hiding place. We didn't think it was a big deal to play with matches. Nothing seemed really bad about them. We would just sit in the middle of the kitchen, away from anything flammable, and light them. Every now and then Christopher would burn some toilet paper for fun, but we always put the asks in a glass cup, or in one of his parent's ash trays. I didn't think anything was going to happen to his house or to Christopher, or to his parents. (BEAT) But something DID happen. Christopher's house was on the news one night. There were a lot of fire trucks outside in the front yard, and smoke was coming from house. T.V. reporters said that everyone inside the house was alive, but the little boy was in critical care. (BEAT) That little boy was Christopher. I almost lost my best-friend to a fire because he was playing with matches. He is alive, I mean, he is okay but ... he won't ever LOOK like Christopher again ... NEVER again. I don't want to touch or even SEE another match for the rest of my life.

Time: Approximately 1 minute 13 seconds

Age Range: 7 – 11

VOCABULARY:

1. <u>matches</u>- small sticks with sulfur tips which are used to make fire

2. <u>flammable</u>- something that can catch on fire easily

3. <u>critical care</u>- an section of a hospital used to take care of people who have been badly injured

Notes

WHAT'S UP WITH GROWN-UPS?
Female   Comedic

••

(Performed as though she is doing stand-up comedy)

What's up with grown-ups anyway? I mean, take my mother
… please. (PAUSE) They always think they're right. Don't they?
My Aunt Rachael tells me to clean my room. I say, "But Aunt
Rachael, I cleaned my room today already." She says, "Go
clean it again." *(makes a face)* Go clean it again?! What does
she want me to do, mess it all up first, and THEN go ahead
and clean it AGAIN? Ha! Sorry, I've got better things to do.
But seriously now, folks. Fathers. (silence) That should say it all.
My dad comes up to me and says, "Oh! Pumpkin, pumpkin,
Hiiii. Do you want a doll? Do you want some ice-cream?" Then
he'll hear the NFL theme song from the other room, and all of
sudden he says, "Gotta-go!" What's up with that? I want my
doll in my lap while I eat ice-cream, but then football takes
its role as the "Important One". Like I'm not as entertaining as
a bunch of oversized little boys playing a game that I figured
out when I was two. You see the ball coming, you catch it. Big
deal. Run with the ball to the side that gives you 6 points. Kick
the ball between two posts, you get more points. I can do all
that and look a lot cuter than the ugly guys with missing teeth
on the T.V. (PAUSE) Okay, so maybe some of them aren't THAT
ugly, but you know what I mean. Just don't get me started on
Uncle Jeff, he's into GOLF.

Time: Approximately 1 minute 15 seconds

Age Range: 8 – 10

VOCABULARY:

1. <u>entertaining</u>- something that is enjoyable
2. <u>oversized</u>- something that is bigger than it should or needs
   to be
3. <u>folks</u>- another way of sating "people"

Tested by kids!

Notes

GOOD-BYE CASTLE
Female   Dramatic

....

My dad built our castle. It's the most beautiful castle in the world. He told me he built it just for me, and as long as we were there nothing bad would ever happen. There were so many rooms to explore and play in. I'd take my dolls up the steps, and pretend they were climbing a mountain because of how high the steps were. They would drive in their pink convertibles up an down the hallways like they were going on a long trip to Japan, or somewhere far that takes a whole lot of driving. But my dolls liked the castle more than me because they couldn't hear mommy and daddy fight. That's the good thing about dolls; they can't hear people fight, they only hear nice things. My grandma told me that mommy and daddy would stop fighting and that everything would get better soon. She said that because we all lived in the magical castle daddy built, and the fighting would HAVE to stop. (PAUSE) I left the castle with my mommy and my little brother one night when daddy wasn't home. The stars were out and they made the nighttime really bright. I tired not to cry, but when I turned around to see the castle one last time, I knew I would never go back. I cried a little bit. But I also knew that we would be okay, because even if we all didn't live in the castle anymore, my daddy and mommy would still love my little brother and me. And that's all that really matters.

Time: Approximately 1 minute 5 seconds

Age Range: 8 – 10

VOCABULARY:

1. <u>explore</u>- to check out places you've never been before

2. <u>convertible</u>- a car whose hood can come off

3. <u>Japan</u>- a country that is also an island, located in Asia

Notes

LOVEY-DOVEY
Male   Comedic

••

Do you know that I despise ... absolutely DESPISE the way my sister acts around her boyfriend? Let's just say it's scary. One minute she'll be kicking me out of the living room while I'M trying to watch my show, but as soon as BRIAN shows up it's all, "Oh! My sweet, adorable little brother. Would you like the remote?" So, of course, I get a little weirded out and run in the opposite direction. Casey gets this odd look on her face just before Brian is at the front door. She is like a female version of <u>Jeckle and Hyde</u>, only worse. You can actually witness the transformation occurring before your very eyes: The little bit of intelligence she has in her brain leaks out of her ears, and she gets this permanent dumb look on her face, like she's some sort of mannequin. But I can deal with the unheard of kindness and the stupid looks. What I can NOT stand is the foul language. You know what I'm talking about. The, "Oh Brian, you're my boo-boo sminerkins." Or, "Schnoocums! You didn't HAVE to buy me this huge bouquet of flowers! Don't EVER buy me anything again!" Then Brian says, "Lovey-dove! But I'd be so SAD not to spend all my money on you!" (*Looks at audience, rolls eyes*) So all this goofy love-talk is what I have to deal with. I'm telling you right now, you'll never catch me saying anything CLOSE to that icky stuff. Really, I'm not going to waste my time, or my parent's money on a girl. Ever. Eww.

Time: Approximately 1 minute 22 seconds

Age Range: 8 – 12

VOCABULARY:

1. <u>despise</u>- to dislike something a LOT

2. <u>version</u>- something that is like something else that came before it. For example, I bought the newest version of an ipod last week

3. <u>transformation</u>- to change dramatically from one thing to another

Notes

NO MORE CANDY
Female   Comedic

....

Halloween is the best. You get to dress up and be anything you like. Last year I went as Cinderella and looked ravishing in my costume. When I went trick-or-treating, the neighbors said things like, "Oh, how adorable! Here, take an extra candy bar, just because you're cute". Ha, ha! Oh, I love that one. I get free extra candy just because I'm cute. But extra candy and extra cuteness comes with a price. They have their downfalls, believe me. There was SO much candy when I got home that I didn't know what to do with myself. I decided the most rational thing to do would be to start with the gummies and end with the chocolate. Mom saw me chowing down and said that I shouldn't eat too much right away because I'd get sick. But at that time, who was caring about getting sick? Not me. I gobbled more than half my candy down, but had to stop at the bon-bons because I had a funny feeling in my belly. By bedtime I thought the end of my life was before me. I felt like I was going to PUKE! My mom MADE me go to school the next day too, even though I wasn't feeling well AT ALL. I visited the nurse's office TWICE and mom still wouldn't let me come home. She said, "That's what you get for not listening to me about the candy!" The remainder of my Halloween candy sat on the counter for weeks until dad threw it away just after Thanksgiving. I was so sick of candy I couldn't even LOOK at gummies until Christmas! Next Halloween I'm going as a goblin so that maybe I'll get LESS candy instead of EXTRA.

Time: Approximately 1 minute 26 seconds.

Age Range: 7 – 11

VOCABULARY:

1. ravishing- absolutely BEAUTIFUL!!

2. gobbled- to eat something too fast

3. through- to be completely done with something

Notes

VIDEOGAME WIZARD
Male   Comedic

••

(*phone rings*) Hello? (BEAT) Yes, this IS Aaron. Are you interested in our stock of over 3 million video games? All video games are new AND improved, and all made by the one, the only, AARON MACKGRAVE! (BEAT) Who? (BEAT) Oh, hi Aunt Rosa. (BEAT) No, I LOVED the pink pillow you made for me last Christmas. (*Makes a weird face*) Yes, well, the holidays are so busy! It was hard to get in touch with you to tell you how lovely the pink duck pillow really is. (BEAT) Yes, I Do realize It's July, but ... (BEAT) Ugh-huh (*quickly*) Well, mom isn't here right now so she'll call you back, bye! (*hangs up quickly*) Aaggh. Gross! (*phone rings*) Hello! This is Aaron Mackgrave here with "Videogame Wizard Etc." How may I help-(BEAT) Nooo! I didn't hang up on you, Aunt Rosa! It must have been a bad connection. These silly cell phones nowadays! (BEAT) Yes, I WILL tell my mom you called. (BEAT) I love you ... too? (BEAT) Yeah, okay, bye. (*hangs up phone*). (*Phone rings*) She doesn't know when to quit. (*Picks up phone*) AUNT ROSA, I didn't hang up on you, you SAID goodbye. (BEAT) Oh. (*Deep voice*) Hey, Rodger, what's up? (BEAT) Sure, ugh, I have over 3 million videogames in stock for you to choose from. (BEAT) WHAT kind? (BEAT) Well, um, I GUESS I could make one with pinks ducks running away from crazy family members. (PAUSE) Actually, I have the PERFECT villain for the game already. (*smile and nods at the audience*)

Time: Approximately 1 minute 18 seconds

Age Range: 8+

VOCABULARY:

1. <u>interested</u>- to want to learn more about something

2. <u>etc.</u>- an abbreviation of etcetera, which means "and other things"

3. <u>villain</u>- the antagonist ("bad guy")

Notes

BOYS DROOL
Female   Comedic

....

(The actor holds a large picture in her hand, 8x11 preferred, which the audience does not see until the specified moment. The picture is of a boy's face with the name "Steve" written largely at the top. There are 15 medium sized hearts drawn all over the picture.)

Boys are so disgusting. They DROOL for crying-out-loud! There is this one boy in particular, Steve, who is in my homeroom class. He drools on his desk every single day. He'll put his head down to go to sleep, and when he wakes up there is a huge puddle of drool all over the place. It grosses me out. Boys also stink. When Steve comes back inside from recess he is a complete stink-pot. I tell him, "Steve, if you didn't have cooties, I'd get close enough to tell you what you REALLY smell like, because from here you're stench is worse then a garbage can left in the middle of New York City, on a rainy day in mid-summer." (BEAT) Boys in general are like one large garbage heap anyway. When they're all together in their little groups, they're like walking, talking, HUGE sewage plants! *(On the word "HUGE", she throws her arms out to reveal the large picture of Steve.)* Oh...um, ha, ha, I can explain. These hearts here represent the level of "stinkiness" that Steve is prone to having. So, if each heart represents a level of "stinkiness" at 10 degrees each, then his PERSONAL level of "stikiness" is 150 degrees. (PAUSE) I should probably change the hearts to stars or check marks or something less conspicuous.

Time: Approximately 1 minute 5 seconds

Age Range: 8 – 11

VOCABULARY:

1. <u>stench</u>- a smell that is not pleasant
2. <u>heap</u>- a pile of stuff

3. <u>sewage</u>- human waste water that is contained in a certain place underground known as a sewer

4. <u>prone</u>- likely to have or get something

Notes

_____

_____

_____

_____

_____

_____

_____

_____

_____

_____

_____

_____

_____

_____

_____

_____

_____

_____

_____

_____

_____

_____

_____

_____

_____

_____

_____

_____

_____

_____

I FORGOT MY LINES!
Male   Dramatic

· ·

We had a play at school the other day and my part was being the toy soldier. It was a Christmas play. I don't know why we put on a Christmas play in the middle of May, but Miss. Angel said we had to because there was a good moral to the story, and she couldn't find another play that had a good moral for kids. "Trash is what the others were!" … that's what she would say. Well, she is a little crazy, so who knows what plays she was reading, but they were probably fine. Anyway, my older sister Zoey was in the play too, and she got the lead role, as usual. SHE was the toy angel. She always impresses a crowd. Audiences LOVE her. The school crowd thought she was the best thing in the world. The more I watched my sister the more nervous I got. I wanted everyone to love ME as much as they seemed to love her. I only had to say one line. Just one stinky little line. "Yes, angel, as a soldier, I agree completely." That was it. The moment was approaching when it was going to be my turn to speak. Do you think I could manage to spit out that one measly little line? Do YA? (BEAT) No. I blew it. I stood there mortified before my audience. I had to put my head down so no one would see me crying like a little girl. Zoey saved the moment by jumping in front of me and asked the clown if he agreed. But in a way that made me feel worse. (PAUSE) I don't think acting is for me anyway. I'm much better at playing sports and video games. At least I don't need to talk when I'm playing THOSE.

Time: Approximately 1 minute 30 seconds

Age Range: 7 – 10

VOCABULARY:

1. <u>moral</u>- a word that represents the rules of "good behavior" in certain societies
2. <u>approaching</u>- to come upon something

3. <u>impress</u>- to please someone else by showing off an ability

4. <u>mortified</u>- to be very embarrassed about something

Notes

_____

_____

_____

_____

_____

_____

_____

_____

_____

_____

_____

_____

_____

_____

_____

_____

_____

_____

_____

_____

_____

_____

_____

_____

_____

_____

_____

_____

_____

_____

_____

_____

_____

_____

_____

SOMEONE ELSE TO BLAME
Female   Comedic

••

I always get blamed by my big sisters for THEIR mistakes. It is always "Jeannie spilled this", or "Jeannie made me do that". But REALLY, it's not true. None of it. The worst part is though, my parents believe them. So after taking this abuse from the older monsters, for oh … 3 years now, I decided things are going to change around here. I may be younger, I may be littler, but I AM smarter! So what I did was set up our video camera and hid it behind the bookshelf, just out of my older sisters' sight, ready to catch one of them in a lie about me. Right when Becca came in the living room, I hit the remote to record and caught her spilling chocolate milk all over mom's white linen that was laid out to iron. Becca ran to my mom as fast as she could and said, "Mommy, Mommy! Jeannie spilled chocolate milk all over your linen!" Heidi, who wasn't even THERE, came in after her with, "Yeah, ugh huh! I SAW HER, she DID it!" My mom was fuming. She looked at me and said , "How is it you're so calm about all this, Jeannie? You don't look a bit sorry for what you've done." I said, "Well, darling mother, that is because I didn't do it." Mom said, "Now, Jeannie, what have we discussed about lying?" That's when I held up the little tape and said, "Oh, I know mommy, and you're absolutely right. I feel that Becca and Heidi need to have a lesson on lying too. So I have the tape of Becca spilling the chocolate milk RIGHT HERE to help you with that." (she smiles broadly)

Time: Approximately 1 minute 28 seconds

Age Range: 8+

VOCABULARY:

1. <u>blame</u>- to point fingers at someone when something went wrong

2. <u>abuse</u>- to treat another person or animal with cruelty

3. <u>discuss</u>- to talk about a certain topic

4. <u>linen</u>- cloth; usually used for bedding or curtains

Tested by kids!

Notes

_____

_____

_____

_____

_____

_____

_____

_____

_____

_____

_____

_____

_____

_____

_____

_____

_____

_____

_____

_____

_____

_____

_____

_____

_____

_____

GIRLS ARE GROSS
Male   Comedic

....

(Actor speaks in a Brooklyn accent throughout the piece)

This girl Miriam kissed me today. Right on my cheek. She had her birthday party at Tony Russo's, everyone's favorite pizza place. I was having a good time, too. I mean, you know, before the tragedy occurred. We was all eatin' pizza, playin' some party games, just casually hangin' out, you know? So I go up to this video arcade thing, right? And I'm mindin' my own business just playin' the game, and Miriam comes up to me and says, "Here goes nothing", and she KISSES me. Just *(puckers up lips)* muah! Like that. Kisses me like I'm some poodle or somethin'. I just looked at her and said, "Hey, babe. Don't do that again, alright? You's is messin' up my game." Don't get me wrong, I don't care if my grandma, or mudda kisses me ... just don't want no gross GIRLS kissin' me, that's all. Now I guess these other girls are like comin' up to me and stuff like they want to kiss me, too. Ugh, I don't think so, ladies. I just wanna play my game and eat my pizza and forget about it. So if any of you's girls are out there listenin' to this, then you know not to mess, 'cause I might just decide to tell your mudda!

Time: Approximately 1 minute 2 seconds

Age Range: 8+

VOCABULARY:

1. <u>tragedy</u>- when something happens that is really, truly awful

2. <u>casually</u>- to be relaxed and comfortable

3. <u>poodle</u>- a type of breed of dog

4. <u>mudda</u>- a silly way of spelling "mother" to help you pronounce the word the way the author intended it to sound

Notes

MY FAMILY VACATION
Female   Comedic

....

Okay Miss. Wensing, this is my report. I hope you like it. (BEAT) On our family vacation last year we went to England. We got to see a lot of famous places that people always talk about like Liverpool, Cambridge, and Stonehenge. Stonehenge was so amazing! My sister is convinced that aliens put the stones there. I said, "Yeah. You think aliens put the stones there because you are FROM outer space!" My sister didn't really take that as an insult. She is really ... different. We also went to London. My dad grew up there and we went to visit his old house and school to see where he used to live. While we were there, a huge carnival came to town. They had animals that you could feed, and rides you could ride, and ice-cream booths set up with every flavor ice-cream you can think of! I decided I wanted to get in line for an elephant ride with mommy, while my dad and sister went off to see a space exhibit. Right when it was my turn to ride the elephant, Bo-Bo decided that he was going to snatch my mom's hat right off her head. Oh, Bo-Bo is the name of the elephant I was supposed to ride. The owner tired bribing him with peanuts to give the hat back, but Bo-Bo really liked my mother's bright magenta hat. Well, the rest of the line was getting impatient so the owner asked if we could get out pictures taken with Bo-Bo, instead of riding him. We agreed, but I didn't want to 'cause I wanted to ride Bo-Bo. My mother never got her hat back, either. She was given 20 quid to buy a new hat, though. The picture of us with Bo-Bo is in our living room. I'm not smiling in it, but mom is because Bo-Bo put his trunk on her head right when the camera snapped! And THAT was my family vacation this year.

Time: Approximately 1 minute 35 seconds

Age Range: 8+

VOCABULARY:

1. <u>convinced</u>- to be completely sure of something
2. <u>insult</u>- to speak to someone with disrespect or abuse
3. <u>impatient</u>- to become frustrated or quickly angered
4. <u>quid</u>- slang for a pound, which is the name of the British currency

Tested by kids!

Notes

_____
_____
_____
_____
_____
_____
_____
_____
_____
_____
_____
_____
_____
_____
_____
_____
_____
_____
_____
_____
_____
_____
_____
_____
_____
_____
_____
_____

OLD FOLKS HOME
Male   Dramatic

....

My dad makes me go visit my grandparents in the old people's home every Saturday afternoon. It is SO boring! I always think about what I could be doing instead of sitting there, in that smelly, moldy place. I could be outside playing some games with my friends, or playing the new video game I just bought. Geeze, I would even rather go GOLFING with my dad than listen to grandpap tell the story about, (mocking) "the time when he was in the War, and the girls would sing him the song about everybody's favorite solider". He tells that story EVERY time I visit. Dad says it makes my grandparents happy to see me. He says at least I have the chance to go home and have a good change of scenery, which is a privilege they don't have anymore. I come back every week to see them, and there they are, right where I left them the week before. (BEAT) I guess he's right, you know? It is good that we get to see each other every week. I just wish we could all go somewhere else rather than sit under those florescent lights and have to smell the mold in the wall. My grandparents deserve better than that. If I could, I'd take them back to my place to live. (PAUSE, sadly) But it doesn't seem like that's going happen.

Time: Approximately 1 minute 10 seconds

Age Range: 8+

VOCABULARY:

1. <u>moldy</u>- mold is a fungus that grows in damp places

2. <u>florescent lights</u>- lights that flicker so fast it looks like they're one solid light; they usually use up less energy than a regular, standard light bulb, are very bright, but they might not be good for certain people's eyes

3. <u>deserve</u>- to show qualities worthy of reward

Notes

DON'T BELIEVE EVERYTHING YOU HEAR
Female   Dramatic

···

Hi, it's me. The new girl. (BEAT) I just wanted to tell you something since you were the first friend ... the first friend-LY person to me at this school. (BEAT) I guess I just want to say ... I'm sorry. I was wrong about you. You are a great person, no matter what anyone else says. (BEAT) I wish I would have known that sooner than now. Nicole said that I should stay away from you. So did a few other people. They said you were "bad news". But I shouldn't have believed them. (BEAT) They're nice enough to ME ... I'd even say they are my friends, but ... (PAUSE) Well, you were the first person to smile at me, and talk to me and ask me questions that you really seemed to care about. You wanted to know what it is like to be home-schooled, and how I had to take my tests, and how I was graded. And I really wanted to know about you, too! About what it was like to go to a public school all your life, and where you lived and what you like to do for fun. (BEAT) I wanted to go ice-skating with you a few weeks ago when you asked me, but Nicole said I shouldn't. She said that it wouldn't make me look so good. (BEAT) I'm sorry, Chelsea, I really am. I guess I shouldn't believe everything I hear. I hope you can accept my apology.

Time: Approximately 1 minute 9 seconds

Age Range: 8+

VOCABULARY:

1. <u>believe</u>- to think something is true
2. <u>seem</u>- to think something may be one way, but might be another
3. <u>apology</u>- saying you're sorry

Notes

THE DIVORCE
Anyone   Dramatic

....

My parents are splitting up. The real word for splitting up is "divorce". (PAUSE) They always fight anyway, so I guess it's better for them to split. They're never nice to each other. I can't think of one time when they WERE nice to each other. Dad has really bad problem with drinking too much alcohol. It makes him REALLY mean and grumpy. He got fired from his job when he showed up late to work too many times. Mom said she was tired of working two jobs just to put food on the table. Dad would use half of her money anyway to buy his beer. Mom told him to get a job and quit drinking or she was going somewhere else to live. (BEAT) Dad did okay for little while. He went to special classes that help people stop drinking. (BEAT) You know it's called an addiction. The problem my dad has, I mean. (slowly) An "addiction". He got a new job, but lost it in less than a month. He's back to the same way he always was. Dad argued with mom for a few nights after he got fired for the fourth time, and mom was getting tired of it. Me and my brother were scared, but we were tired of it too. One night my mom locked him out of the house and that was the last time he tired to come back. Well, actually, he TRIED to come back in, but mom called Grandma and Grandpap, who called the police. All of them showed up at the same time, and the police put daddy in their car and drove him off to jail with the lights flashing. That's when mom told my brother and me that her and dad were splitting up. I really don't mind, though. Divorce can be a bad thing, but I think for us it's not going to be as bad as my parents staying together.

Time: Approximately 1 minute 30 seconds

Age Range: 8+

VOCABULARY:

1. <u>divorce</u>- when a married couple separate from each other legally

2. <u>addiction</u>- when someone loses the ability to control themselves from NOT doing a certain thing, like drinking alcohol

3. <u>argue</u>- when people verbally fight with one another

Notes

THE FLOOD
Female   Dramatic

There were these girls I heard talking in the mall today. They were a little older than me, but I still think the way they were talking was ridiculous. One girl was saying to the others, "I hate my parents, they never let me buy ANYTHING I want." The other girls agreed with her and kept complaining about how they were, (imitating the girls voices) "Only allowed to buy one outfit a week because we have to learn RESPONSIBILITY. Ha, WHATEVER! All I know is I need to new fuchsia outfit because fuchsia is the new black." (BEAT) They KEPT talking like that, and all I wanted to do was go up to them and say they never had to KNOW. They probably will never HAVE to know. They won't know the way it feels to lose an entire house to a flood. (BEAT) All my things, my pictures, my toys, my bedroom that my grandma painted for me ... it's all gone forever. It was there one minute, and in less than five minutes it's like it never was. So terrifying. (PAUSE) My family was rescued, and we're all alive, so I'm thankful for THAT. But the PAIN is unlike anything those girls will ever know about. They'll worry about whether or not they'll wear a fuchsia blouse on their next date, NOT what they'll be wearing for the next six months to school. My clothes are all gone except for what I had on my back, and what's been donated to me from the rescue society, just so I had something ... ANYTHING to wear. It'd be nice to buy one new outfit a week. It'd be GREAT to be mad at my parents for spoiling me just enough to know that I'm spoiled. But that's not REAL. Those girls at the mall today live in a great fantasy world, and I'd be kidding myself if I thought I could be like them for one second. The memories of the flood will ALWAYS haunt me, and remind me of who I REALLY am, and what REALLY matters in this world. (PAUSE) I'll never forget it.

Time: Approximately 1 minute 50 seconds

Age Range: 9+

VOCABULARY:

1. <u>ridiculous</u>- to be silly, but usually in an unattractive way
2. <u>imitate</u>- to copy someone or something exactly
3. <u>fuchsia</u>- a shade of pink; a bright pinkish-purple color
4. <u>terrifying</u>- something that is absolutely frightful

Notes

_____
_____
_____
_____
_____
_____
_____
_____
_____
_____
_____
_____
_____
_____
_____
_____
_____
_____
_____
_____
_____
_____
_____
_____
_____
_____
_____

TRADITION
Anyone   Dramatic

••

We celebrate the winter holidays the same way every year. On Christmas Eve my brothers and I are allowed to open one present each while we watch a Christmas special on television. We'll make homemade buttermilk cookies from my great-great grandmother's secret recipe, and then leave them out for Santa. This is all part of our Christmas tradition. It is so much fun because we have many, many things to do, and look forward to doing. I also love going to visit our aunt's house on Christmas Eve night, just before we go out to midnight mass at Church. All the family goes to my aunt's place to eat dinner together. (BEAT) This Christmas will be a little different, though. My pap-pap would always read, "The Night Before Christmas" at my aunt's house. But earlier this year, my pap-pap passed away. My Uncle Amadeo will read the story this year, but it will be sad not to have pap-pap reading the book. That was part of our tradition. His voice was so jolly when he read. He sounded just like Santa when he shouted, "Merry Christmas to all, and to all a good night!" (PAUSE, *thinking fondly*) Pap-pap will be there this year in spirit. The only difference is that Uncle Amadeo isn't pap-pap, but it's okay because the tradition will still live on, and THAT is what matters. Pap-pap would want it this way. (*Smiles*)

Time: Approximately 1 minute 16 Seconds

Age Range: 7 – 10

VOCABULARUY:

1. recipe- instructions for cooking certain foods
2. tradition- customs or beliefs passed down from generation to generation
3. Midnight Mass- in the Christian religion, some churches have a service at midnight to celebrate the birth of Jesus Christ

Notes

MY LITTLE BROTHER IS SPECIAL
Female   Dramatic

My little brother Ryan is really special. He is blind which means he can't see. But please don't think that means he's dumb, or incapable of doing things, because he's the smartest boy I know. Ryan sings beautiful songs that he makes up on the piano. Right now he's teaching me how to play, but I can't play nearly as good as he can. He just ... (*thinks for a moment*) he KNOWS what music sounds likes before he starts to play a song. Mom wants to buy him lessons but dad thinks he should keep making up his own music. Dad taught him the names of the keys and that's all Ryan needs to know in order to write his own music. Ryan's so smart and I'm so proud to be his big sister. Even though he's blind he sees things that I and regular, ordinary people can't see. (PAUSE) He SEES the music. Someday Ryan will be famous for his music. He's going to be amazing ... he already is amazing to me.

Time: Approximately 1 minute

Age Range: 7+

VOCABULARY:

1. <u>incapable</u>- not able to do something

2. <u>ordinary</u>- another way of saying "normal"

3. <u>piano keys</u>- the long black and white planks on a piano that you press to play music

Notes

STAGE FRIGHT!
Anyone   Comedic

··

Wow. Okay. There are a LOT of people out there, Miss. Williams, I don't think I can do this. I realize I'm a great singer; YOU know I'm a great singer; all the other kids in the talent show know I'm a great singer. I just never thought the audience would be so ... so ... HUGE. Since the people that really matter know I'm awesome, like my family, friends, and YOU, why don't you say we call this a day? (BEAT) Yeah, but just looking at the audience gives me butterflies! I feel like I'm on this constant roller coaster and the feeling never dissipates! (BEAT) What? (BEAT) What do you mean I can't quit now? There is NO WAY I'm about to go out there and sing. What if I forget how? Or what if I go to sing and my notes come out sounding like garbage? (BEAT) Just pretend like the seats are empty? You mean like they have been? (PAUSE) Hmmm. That's not such a bad idea. If I THINK no one is watching me, then maybe I'll do even better than I did in rehearsal. I do the best job when I'm in my room by myself. Do you really think pretending the seats are empty will help me out? (PAUSE) Maybe since I can SEE people out there, I'll just pretend they aren't REAL people, what do you think? I mean as though they're all on a bunch of mannequins or something. (PAUSE) Thank you, Miss. Williams. No one in the seats at all. Just a bunch of mannequins. This will be piece of cake!

Time: Approximately 1 minute 15 seconds

Age Range: 8+

VOCABULARY:

1. <u>constant</u>- something that happens over and over again; it never stops, it's always there

2. <u>dissipates</u>- to scatter and disappear

3. <u>concerned</u>- to be worried

Tested by kids!

Notes

_____

_____

_____

_____

_____

_____

_____

_____

_____

_____

_____

_____

_____

_____

_____

_____

_____

_____

_____

_____

_____

_____

_____

_____

_____

_____

_____

_____

_____

_____

_____

_____

_____

_____

_____

_____

_____

_____

SCHOOL BLUES
Female   Comedic

••

School can really get a girl down. Look at me! I'm a wreck! I get up at 7 in the morning and work all day at school. You think LIFE in the OFFICE is bad? You grown-ups don't know how easy you've got it. At 9:00am sharp I do spelling. Who wants to worry about the difference between their, there, and they're at 9 in the MORNING? Then, THEN as soon as 9:30am hits, its' (shudders) MATH. M-A-T-H, math. Yeah, times tables in the morning. By 11:00, my tummy feels like a never-ending pit, and I could eat the first pig that walks past me. The next thing you know, some teacher who fancies themselves an artist, sticks a piece of paper in front of you and cup of dried beans and tells you to throw something nice together to make your parents happy! (PAUSE) I don't know about you, but it takes a lot more than dried beans and recycled newspaper to make MY parents happy. (Deep sigh) My mom and dad have the nerve to tell me school isn't as bad as work. A grown-up's day ENDS at 5 PM. School, however, follows kids home with at least 3 hours of homework a night. No wonder kids are getting more and more stressed out as generations pass. We're worked day and night like slaves by THE SYSTEM. (PAUSE) I REALLY could use a T.V. break right about now. Because just talking about school gets me anxious.

Time: Approximately 1 minute 17 seconds

Age Range: 8+

VOCABULARY:

1. <u>differences</u>- a way in which people or things are not alike

2. <u>fancies</u>- someone who believes they are one thing, but might actually not be

3. <u>generations</u>- one generation equals 10 years; example: 1950-1960 is one generation, 1980-1990 is another generation

Notes

T.V. ISN'T FOR EVERYONE
Anyone   Comedic

....

My friends think I'm weird because I don't like to watch T.V. They'll be in school talking about what they saw on Sunday night T.V., or Tuesday afternoon T.V., or THURSDAY morning T.V., but I just don't see the appeal. I've even tried to sit down and watch a cartoon or two. I tried REALLY hard to like it, but I just can't get into television. I'd honestly rather sit on my bed and pull out a book or two that I've been reading. I have more fun finding out what will happen at the end of a chapter, than waiting to see what happens at the end of a 20-minute cartoon, that doesn't even have a point to a story. Seriously, a cartoon is just a drawing with some real person's voice dubbed-in trying to sound like an animal that talks. (BEAT) The whole concept kind of scares me, actually. But just because the majority of people like to watch T.V., doesn't mean I think THEY are weird, so why do they have to think I'M weird? Just because I don't like T.V. doesn't mean I'm some side-show exhibit. It just means I have better things to do with my time than sit in front of a box and fry my brain all day, everyday. (BEAT) That probably explains why my brother is so spacey.

Time: Approximately 1 minute

Age Range: 8+

VOCABULARY:

1. <u>appeal</u>- something that is attractive or interesting
2. <u>dubbed</u>- when a person's voice is used to give the cartoon the appearance of speaking
3. <u>concept</u>- an idea
4. <u>exhibit</u>- to display something in a formal manner

Notes

RULES OF THE FAMOUS
Anyone   Comedic

....

(Recommended for staged reading)

(Calling to someone off-stage) How much time, Lucy? (PAUSE) Thanks, love! *(To the audience)* Wow, the first day on the set! You gotta love being a movie star. Everyone treats you like royalty around here. Fan mail comes pouring in everyday, and people ALWAYS want your autograph. When you're famous, and you're out in public, SMILE at the paparazzi. THEY are the people who exploit you to the world, and they are the real reason why you will STAY famous. My mom told me all about it. The more you smile, and the friendlier you are, the more the world adores your every move. Don't worry if the tabloids say things like, "Famous child star gets caught in the act of stealing cookies from famous director" ... because it's rumors like that which will make people MORE interested in you. They will want to see your films even MORE than before! Now, don't get me wrong. You don't have to be FRIENDS with everyone, but you do have to be friend-LY. No one likes to mingle or even WORK with a snot-nosed, I-think-I'm-better-than-you brat; BE charming. Lure their love with your gracious smile, and polite behavior. Be witty, but don't over do it. Show off your cute personality, but don't let them think YOU KNOW you're cute, even though you do. ALWAYS look your best, but pretend like you're not paying attention to what you wear. And last but not least, when you get your paychecks, don't go over-spending it at the mall. Invest in Swiss Banks with high interest rates with at least 55% of your income. Put another 25% into college savings, and then use the rest at your own disposal. Believe me, if you want to stay wealthy in THIS industry, you better start saving the minute you're making. (PAUSE) OH! I gotta run. Have a production meeting with my agent and manager and a few producers for my up-coming film, but we'll do lunch, just have your people call my people. Ciao darlings!

Time: Approximately 1 minute 50 seconds

Age Range: 8+

VOCABULARY:

1. <u>autograph</u>- a famous person's signature
2. <u>paparazzi</u>- photographers who follow stars and invade their space to make money off their image
3. <u>exploit</u>- to make full use of something and get a benefit from it (in this case, the paparazzi use pictures of stars to make money)
4. <u>ciao</u>- this is an Italian word that means "good-bye"; it is pronounced like "chow"

Notes

THE DREAM?
Anyone   Comedic

••

Last night, I had the craziest dream. I dreamt that I went to my window and saw a lime-green flying car, with little fur balls driving it … or flying it, rather. When a fur ball honked the horn, the horn sang my name: "Tay-lor! Tay-lor!" They flew over to me, and said, "What's up?" I replied, "Not much. Sooo … where did you buy that car?" They answered, "We'll tell you if you come inside and share some of this delicious homemade iced tea with us." So naturally I put on some socks and flew out my window. Inside the car, there was more room than you would think. The inside of the car was as large as my living room! The car continued to grow into this HUGE flying 50's diner, where one of the fur balls on roller skates came up to me with a lifetime supply of bubble gum and a glass of purple iced tea. Well, let me tell you this was the BEST iced tea I've ever had. Plus, it was glowing purple! Awesome. The fur balls call themselves Liptonites, from the planet Liptonian, of the solar system Xeonia. They showed me around their ship, which had the capability of changing into whatever was convenient for the Liptonites travel needs. They have the coolest things I've ever seen inside their ship. There was a microwave-type-thingy that cooks an entire five course meal with the push of a button, a machine that can do your homework in less than 5 seconds, and a theme park with every ride imaginable. I had so much fun in this dream, I didn't want to wake up. When I eventually opened my eyes, I was sad about leaving the Liptonites … it seemed so real to me … but it HAD to be a dream … Liptionite people and the planet Liptonian don't exist! (*Puts hand in pocket*) They CAN'T exist … (*takes out a few pieces of bubble gum*) or … CAN they?!

Time: Approximately 2 minutes

Age Range: 9+

VOCABULARY:

1. <u>naturally</u>- another way of saying "of course"
2. <u>capability</u>- the ability to do something
3. <u>convenient</u>- to fit in well with a person's needs

Notes

_____

_____

_____

_____

_____

_____

_____

_____

_____

_____

_____

_____

_____

_____

_____

_____

_____

_____

_____

_____

_____

_____

_____

_____

_____

_____

_____

_____

_____

I'M GOING ON AN AIRPLANE!
Anyone   Comedic

....

(Extreme energy throughout the monologue)

I'm so nervous! I have to go on an airplane for the very first time and … ugh … I can't really say I'm ready for it. Wait! Let me think. (PAUSE, thinks) Nope, no definitely NOT ready for it! I'm supposed to visit my cousins who life in Australia and they just COULDN'T come over HERE. Oh, no, why would they want to do that? I'll tell you why! Because they've already BEEN here at least ten times in the past five years. They've BEEN on airplanes, and they're TIRED of always coming over here. So now, I'm the one who gets to go on the airplane. My mother keeps telling me to calm down and that I'm making her nervous. SHE has room to talk! Me make HER nervous? The lady's been on a million airplanes before. (*Real big*) HAVE SOME SYMPATHY PEOPLE! I will no longer be on the ground in 20 minutes like YOU all! YOU will be comfy cozy on the ground with your precious GRAVITY. Well SUE me for being nervous, okay? (Sarcastically) 'Cause I'm the one who said, "Hey, self! Why don't you go on an airplane ride to AUSTRALIA and drive yourself into a hysterical fit before getting on the plane? – Oh yes, self, that sounds like a GREAT idea!" (PAUSE) Oh-my-gosh. It's time to board. They just called my row. (*Breathes into a paper bag a few times, then says sadly and slowly:*) Enjoy your gravity, people. You don't know how precious it is … until it's gone!

Time: Approximately 1 minute 36 seconds

Age Range: 8+

VOCABULARY:

1. <u>sympathy</u>- feeling sorry for someone else
2. <u>gravity</u>- invisible force that keeps objects on earth grounded, and not floating around
3. <u>hysterical</u>- uncontrolled and extreme emotion

Notes

BROADWAY BOUND
Anyone   Comedic

••

Ah, BROADWAY! Don't ya just love the LIGHTS? The PEOPLE? The FREE FOOD?! Broadway is the place to be, and brother, that's where I'm goin'! I'm tellin' ya, someday I'm gonna be famous. More famous than Barbara, or even Frankie Sanatra! I'll be tapping on piano tops and singing old-time musicals for charity matinees. I'll learn to whistle for cabs to take me to work, and to restaurants and … OH SOHO baby, yeah! That's where my photo shoots will be … or right in front of Central Park. I'm fairly partial to the park. Then home again at night to good ole Greenwich Village. My neighbors will come out nightly to shake my hand, "How are you Mr./Miss.____ ____?" And my reply will be, "OH you know, another morning of coffee shops and interviews, an afternoon of talk shows and a performance in the evening. Same old. And YOU, Daniel? It IS Daniel, right?" (Deep sigh) Oh! To live the life of a famous Broadway star. But you know, it isn't the money I'm after. It ain't the MONEY! It's the ART! I'm going to show New York what a REAL actor can do. I'll give her the boy/girl she's been waitin' for all her life. That city needs me, and Broadway is what will make all that magic possible! I'm going straight to the top! Brothers and sisters, little did you know before you came here tonight that you would have the rare privilege, the RAREST opportunity to see the future-famous, most fabulous Broadway star the world will ever know!

Time: Approximately 1 minute 45 seconds

Age Range: 8+

VOCABULARY:

1. rare- something that does not happen very often

2. matinee- a theatre performance or other live show that takes place during the day, and is usually cheaper than a nighttime show

3. <u>partial</u>- to like something a lot
4. <u>Greenwich</u>- pronounced "Gren-itch", is a section of New York City

Notes

FOOTBALL IS LIFE
Male   Dramatic

....

My dad is SO serious about football. Before my football games start, he makes me wear a relic around my neck, and count to seven, seven times. He thinks that will bring the team good luck, and that I'll play well. I have to run three miles before getting onto my bus in the morning, and I'm only allowed to eat steak and burgers for dinner during the season. Dad says, "It helps you play like a man." Mom gets so worked up about my games that she has to clean the entire house, top to bottom, at LEAST twice. I tell her to chill out, and that it's just a game, but she'll just yell back at me and say, "Don't you DARE let your father hear you say that! Now take it back, I know you didn't mean it." But I DO mean it. Football is really JUST a game. My older brothers play Varsity in high school, and WOW do I feel bad for them. My parents REALLY lash out on them if they lose a game. Dad was a state champion back in college, and so was his younger brother. My mom was an All-State cheerleader, which is how she met dad. Mom cheered for his team, and was there when dad had his fatal game. Oh, I guess I should tell you about that. Yeah, dad broke his leg in a championship game, and ended his career. He had just been drafted to play for the NFL, WHILE he was still a student, so he was really good when he had a better knee. But now he tells me and my brothers that we have the chance he never had. We need to play great and train right in order to be the very best players in the state … he says eventually we'll be the best in the country. (BEAT) Dad and mom are REALLY into the game. Around my house, football IS life.

Time: Approximately 1 minute 34 seconds

Age Range: 9+

VOCABULARY:

1. <u>drafted</u>- when someone is chosen from a large number of people to participate in a task

2. <u>fatal</u>- causes failure or even death

3. <u>varsity</u>- the best group of players for a sport are on the varsity team

Notes

_____
_____
_____
_____
_____
_____
_____
_____
_____
_____
_____
_____
_____
_____
_____
_____
_____
_____
_____
_____
_____
_____
_____
_____
_____
_____
_____
_____
_____
_____
_____
_____

THE PRESENT FROM GRANDMA
Female   Comedic

....

My Grandma Underwood is a sweetheart. She is the sweetest grandma anyone could ask for, truly. But ... she needs a little bit of help with choosing Christmas presents ... at least in making Christmas gifts FAIR. (PAUSE) For Christmas last year, my little brother, who is 3 ½ years YOUNGER than me, got 50 bucks. 50 BUCKS!! He was so excited, he was bouncing off the walls. He bounced off the furniture, bounced off the cat ... he wouldn't stop bouncing. So, naturally, I was excited to see how much money I was going to get. Because since I AM 3 ½ years older than Rew, I should get 3 ½ times as much money, right? Well, Grandma gave me a little wrapped box to open. I thought, "Oh! This is cute! She put my money in a pretty little green box." So I opened the box, and much to my surprise, there was no money, but three pieces of my grandma's pre-used play jewelry. (BEAT) Aaaaand I thought, "Hum." (BEAT) "This must be some mistake." But no. No, that once used PLAY jewelry was MY Christmas gift. I didn't cry or take a fit, as my mother calls it. I just calmly put the box down and said, "Thanks, Gram!", to my sweet, darling, confused grandmother, and left the room to scream into a pillow. (PAUSE to smile) Dad gave me some of Rew's money, so we got $25 each. Next year, dad and mom are going to double-check with grandma to make sure Christmas presents are reasonable, unlike they were LAST year!

Time: Approimately 1 minute 20 seconds

Age Range: 9 – 12

VOCABULARY:

1. <u>bucks</u>- slang for dollars
2. <u>pre-used</u>- something that is not new because someone else used it before giving it to you
3. <u>reasonable</u>- having judgment that is fair and makes sense

Notes

MY DOG DIDN'T REALLY EAT MY HOMEWORK ...
Male   Comedic

....

(Character is very fidgety throughout the piece; clearly shaken)

Hi, Mrs. Zemany? Um, I have a REALLY good reason for not having my homework today. Do you want to hear the story? *(Quickly, without giving her a chance to answer:)* Not that it's a "story" story, but it's an actual thing that happened ... not that you'd THINK I'd tell a "story" story, anyway. (BEAT) Something detrimental happened to me on my way out the door this morning. You see, I did my homework last night like I always do. *(Quickly:)* Not that you'd think I don't always do my homework, 'cause I'm not the type of kid to pay someone else to do it ... not that you'd think I would be, your honor, but just so you know. (BEAT) Um ... anyway, like I was saying, I did ALL my homework and even extra; I did the math, the assigned reading ... which was very poorly structured, by the way. *(Quickly:)* Not that it's YOUR fault, your honor. I understand that YOU didn't write it, and that because of the curriculum you don't have a CHOICE about what we learn. (BEAT) Um, when I was through with all the work, I put it in my backpack and went to bed, you see? Well, my BRILLIANT baby sister hid some doggy-treats in the front pocket of my backpack last night after I went to sleep. She keeps irregular hours. Then, this morning my dog attacked me! I didn't realize what was going on when my dog jumped on my back, and started ripping my pack to shreds. But it turns out the reason he was eating my backpack, along with the homework in it, was because of the doggy-treats. He then promptly threw up the homework along with the doggy-treats because he consumed everything too quickly. I have a note from my parents to confirm these allegations. *(Quickly:)* Not that you'd think I'd LIE to you, but just so you have it on file. And I apologize for making you take up our precious class time to listen to the terrible situation I came to find myself in today. Thank you, your honor.

Time: Approximately 1 minute 50 seconds

Age Range: 9+

VOCABULARY:

1. <u>curriculum</u>- specific materials of subjects that are taught in school
2. <u>consumed</u>- to eat
3. <u>detrimental</u>- tending to cause harm
4. <u>structured</u>- the way something is organized

Notes

_____
_____
_____
_____
_____
_____
_____
_____
_____
_____
_____
_____
_____
_____
_____
_____
_____
_____
_____
_____
_____
_____
_____
_____
_____

GREAT AUNT MARY WEARS A WIG!
Female   Comedic

••

My great-aunt is one of the FANCIEST ladies I know. Her living room, bathroom, and kitchen ALL have at least one sparkling chandelier. Her house never has a spec of dust in it, and it always smells like flowers. Great-Aunty Mary wears outfits that are one color so that her shoes, purse, and jewelry can all match. Her makeup makes her look 20 years younger than she really is, and she sings opera from morning to night. I just love her to bits! (*Dramatic* PAUSE) But then … one day I was horrified. I saw her hair … sitting on … a mannequin! Not just some strands of hair, or even a CHUNK … it was her ENTIRE head of hair sitting there in the perfect, prim, and proper style that it's always in. (*Big breath:*)At first I thought someone had scalped her! But then I realized the horror beyond horror. Great Aunty Mary wears a WIG! I thought this Opera-singer-turned-house-wife spent HOURS making her hair perfect while fixing the rest of her home to be a picturesque Victorian masterpiece. I guess I shouldn't be shocked. I've always been told things aren't always as they seem … ESPECIALLY in operas.

Time: Approximately 1 minute 0 seconds

Age Range: 9+

VOCABULARY:

1. <u>chandelier</u>- a fancy hanging light with branches for several light bulbs

2. <u>horrified</u>- to be really, and truly frightened

3. <u>prim</u>- formal and respectable

4. <u>scalped</u>- historical   reference: the scalp with the hair belonging to it cut or torn away from an enemy's head as a battle trophy

Notes

PICKING ON JIMMY
Male   Dramatic

···

(Based on a true story.)

My teacher has rules posted in our classroom. At the beginning of the school year we would go over them everyday for the first nine weeks. The main three rules are, "No Cheating", "No Bullying", and "No Weapons". Then all the other rules which are after those three aren't as important, like "Raise Your Hand Before Speaking"; things like that. Well, my whole school found out why the three main rules ARE the three main rules. This boy, Jimmy, was in the fifth grade and he got picked on all the time, for no reason! He looked normal, he talked normally … the more I think about it, he really was just a normal guy. But everyone would pick on him for whatever reason they could think of. Maybe they wanted to make THEMSESLVES feel better about who THEY are. I don't know. Jimmy would try so hard to fit in though; he would do anything just to be left alone. Kids would tease him about his sneakers, so he bought different sneakers. They'd say something mean about his hair, so he got a new haircut. Whatever people harassed him about, Jimmy would try to change it. But then one day the biggest bully in the school, Zack is his name, came up behind Jimmy and pushed him over. Jimmy fell right in the middle of the hallway and dropped all his stuff all over the place. He had a drink in one hand, too, and it spilled all over his t-shirt. People were laughing and talking about it for days. I felt so bad for Jimmy. (BEAT) I really wish I would have stood up to Zack, but I was so scared. (BEAT) Jimmy stopped coming to school after that. People began wondering where he went, but even the teachers didn't know what happened to Jimmy. Word got around that he moved to a new school to avoid being teased at this one. It's sad that he had to move, but what else could he do? He tried everything, and no one helped him. Not even the teachers. The teachers were THERE, they heard EVERYTHING … but never said a word. (BEAT) "No Bullying" is a rule that should be enforced more often at my school.

Time: Approximately 2 minutes

Age Range: 9+

VOCABULARY:

1. <u>posted</u>- to display something on paper for everyone to see
2. <u>harassed</u>- to bother someone in a rude manner and on purpose
3. <u>avoid</u>- purposefully keep away from something or someone
4. <u>enforced</u>- to demand and insist that something is done

Notes

_____
_____
_____
_____
_____
_____
_____
_____
_____
_____
_____
_____
_____
_____
_____
_____
_____
_____
_____
_____
_____
_____
_____
_____

SHAMU SHAMPOO FOR YOU! (A COMMERCIAL)
Female   Comedic

••

(Character holds huge bottle, big smile all the way through.)

Ladies, are you tired of the same old shampoo that always lets you down? Perhaps it leaves your hair limp or damaged? Well, fret no more, 'cause I have just the anecdote for you! It's called, "Shamu Shampoo for You!" Your hair will feel healthier, look healthier, and BE healthier in no time. The color will never fade, and will give you more volume than hairspray in the 80's! And you remember 80's hair. Attract the handsomest of men from miles around with this wondrous product! Did I mention the shine? Oh, and gentlemen, don't think we forgot about you. Even if you're bald, we can guarantee your bald head will be silky-smooth, with the kind of shine that radiates through the aisles of the supermarket, making all the lovely ladies giggle with glee. So stop by any store that sells shampoo today to pick up a 68oz bottle of "Shamu Shampoo for You"; on special markdown worldwide for only $1.00 per ounce, that's $1.00 PER OUNCE! Buy today!

Time: Approximately 1 minute

Age Range: 9+

VOCABULARY:

1. <u>perhaps</u>- another way of saying "maybe"
2. <u>fret</u>- to worry
3. <u>wondrous</u>- something wonderful, or unbelievable (but in a GOOD way)
4. <u>markdown</u>- when an item at the store is on sale

Tested by kids!

Notes

STRONG DUDE
Male   Comedic

···

*<u>Note:</u> there are question marks at the end of several sentences To indicate voice inflection. The voice raises naturally when you ask a question. Therefore, raise your voice as you would if you were asking a question when you reach those designated sentences.

If you ever need anything heavy picked up, I'm your dude. Honestly man, one day I woke up and I was the strongest dude in the world. Man, I have picked up the heaviest boulder off my mother's car so that this one tow truck could take it to the dump? Don't ask how the boulder got there, it's like, a long story? But when the tubular toe truck was on its way, it ended up breaking down. I was like, "Man." Mommy was like, "Woah." And I was like, "Yeah." So I took off down the street, and just started runnin' dude. I mean, man, I ran a mile and a half in record time; two minutes flat, to be exact, to reach the tow truck? I picked it up and took it back to the shop where the dude and I got another one so my mommy wasn't stuck waiting all night with like, a smashed car? Now, I may not look like my muscles are capable of lifting a truck or boulder, or house, or rocket ship, but I can dudes … oh, and dude-ettes. But lifting heavy things and being everyone's hero isn't really, like, my passion? I'm actually working on my first career choice which is surfing. Dudes … and dude-ettes … if you're interested in like, suf-lessons, I can like, totally help you out with that, no prob. But yeah, if you need something heavy picked up, I'm still doin' that on the side.

Time: Approximately 1 minute 10 seconds

Age Range: 9+

VOCABULARY:

1. <u>boulder</u>- a big, huge rock

2. <u>capable</u>- the ability to do something
3. <u>designated</u>- specific place, thing, or position

Notes

_____

_____

_____

_____

_____

_____

_____

_____

_____

_____

_____

_____

_____

_____

_____

_____

_____

_____

_____

_____

_____

_____

_____

_____

_____

_____

_____

_____

_____

_____

_____

_____

_____

LIKE, TOTALLY
Female   Comedic

....

(Actor uses a cell phone throughout)

So, um, yeah. I am like totally in love with my new cell phone, Tiff! It's like the newest model by Marcinbrosh and its pink and its pretty ... and, um ... (PAUSE) pretty. Ha! Ha! Ha! (PAUSE) OH! Like totally! I so totally know pink is way in and like stuff. Pink is the new black, girlfriend, don't you know? (PAUSE) WHO did? (PAUSE) Brandon is like THE hottest guy in the class and if he passes you another note or something, you HAVE to text message me! (PAUSE) Oh yeah, girlie! You gotta write him back and tell him you like him, too. He's totally into you and totally wants to take you out. (PAUSE) Yeah, I KNOW I said totally twice, but that's because I REALLY mean it! (PAUSE) What? I can't hear you. (PAUSE) Hello? HELLO?! (PAUSE) Oh, my battery died. (*To audience, suddenly sophisticated*) Cell phones and other forms of modern technology have the tendency to be completely unreliable. A consensus was agreed between my closest acquaintances, e.g. my friends, and myself, and resulted in a unanimous agreement that suggests 1.5 to 3.5 percent of the time a caller's cellular signal drops out, or a battery unexpectedly dies in the middle of a conversation. (BEAT) (*Back to valley-girl mode:*) Whatever! I'll just go recharge this thingy!

Time: Approximately 1 minute 12 seconds

Age Range: 9+

VOCABULARY:

1. <u>tendency</u>- something that happens a lot

2. <u>unanimous</u>- when two or more people agree with each other

3. <u>consensus</u>- general agreement within a group of two or more people

4. <u>acquaintances</u>- someone you know but might not be close friends

Notes

_____
_____
_____
_____
_____
_____
_____
_____
_____
_____
_____
_____
_____
_____
_____
_____
_____
_____
_____
_____
_____
_____
_____
_____
_____
_____
_____
_____

GET ME OUT OF THIS SCHOOL!
Anyone   Comedic

••

(Paranoid and a little frantic, but controlled)

Oh man. Man oh man. *(Taps finger on desk/table)* Come on, clock. I've been sitting here for more than half my life now. At least that's how I feel. You've been at 2:49 for 17 minutes. Can you please change? Change. Change! Go BACKWARDS for goodness sake, but at least CHANGE! Oh thank GOD! 2:50 PM. Okay, okay. I can do this. Okay. 2:50 PM. One big "p" and one big "m", *(quickly)* 2, 5, 0 *(0 is pronounced as "oh", not "zero")* School's not so bad, is it? No. No way. Just takes up more time than I have to sleep at night, but not bad. I have to listen to Ms. Old-Shack grind her teeth in between sentences and watch Kim Teatock pick her nose and eat the boogers, but NOT BAD! *(Getting a little nutty)* Just get to 3:00. *(Pounds the desk with one fist)* C'MON! (PAUSE) Okay, okay 2:58. Good. Good, I'm glad. Yes … as soon as I'm out of this school I can … I can eat some purple ice boxes. No, wait. That doesn't make sense. That didn't make sense at all! This must be … this must be SCHOOL MADNESS! It gets to you. It makes you say crazy things like, " I want to eat purple ice boxes". Am I fat? Answer me! This isn't good … oh! OH! HI Miss. Old-Sha -- … ugh, ALZACK. Ha, ha … how you doin'? WHAT? It's 3:25?! REALLY? Why didn't you wake me up sooner? Oh, yes ma'am, can't WAIT to come back tomorrow. *(Looks at audience, sarcastically nods head)* Oh- yeah.

Time: Approximately 1 minute 25 seconds

Age Range: 9+

VOCABULARY:

1. paranoid- unreasonably anxious or mistrustful
2. frantic- wild with fear or anxiety

3. sarcastically- say or do one thing, but mean something else entirely

Notes

_____

_____

_____

_____

_____

_____

_____

_____

_____

_____

_____

_____

_____

_____

_____

_____

_____

_____

_____

_____

_____

_____

_____

_____

_____

_____

_____

_____

_____

_____

_____

_____

_____

LOVE-SICK
Female   Comedic

....

I don't understand this feeling I have in my belly. It's weird. It feels like I'm having a belly ache, but it's not a real belly ache because I only feel this way when I think about ... Adam. Adam is a boy I really like. He's really cute and nice, and SO cool. I didn't even realize that I liked him until I noticed my belly hurting one day. It started when I saw him laughing with another girl at lunch. I think I actually got jealous of her. So I went over and sat next to them. It ended up being fine, they were just talking about a movie they both saw recently. Adam sits next to me in our reading and science classes. We were partners in those classes when we did group work yesterday. I passed him a note to tell him I liked him. He wrote me back saying he liked me, too. So even though I like him, and he likes me, my belly STILL keeps hurting. Mom says it's puppy love, and the feeling I have in my belly is called love-sickness. (PAUSE, *suddenly cheerful*) So I'm love sick over Adam! I think I'm going to ask him if he wants to be my boyfriend. He'll be my first boyfriend this year! Last year I had one, and the year before that I had three. But I've never felt this way before. It's all new to me ... I wonder if Adam is love sick, too? Maybe I'll ask him.

Time: Approximately 1 minute 15 seconds

Age Range: 10 – 12

VOCABULARY:

1. notice- to pay attention to something in particular
2. jealous- when you wish you had something someone else has, but you want it so much you have ill feelings toward the person who has it (jealousy is NOT a good or nice thing, try not to be jealous of anyone!)
3. serious- something that is very important

Notes

SOCCER'S IN THE FAMILY
Male   Dramatic

....

My family has been playing soccer for centuries. We moved here from Brazil in the early 1900s. That was where my great-grandfather played soccer for a traveling team called "The Warriors", and he became a legend for being the fastest runner on a soccer field in all of Brazil. I'm third generation Brazilian-American, and the tradition of playing soccer is still alive in my family. My grand-pap, dad, and uncles all played soccer for years and years. My three older brothers play soccer, too. Their teams play like their LIVES depend on it. Soccer is the air they breathe. I'd be the same way except my team isn't in the high school yet, so people aren't as excited about it ... which includes both the players and our audience. But that doesn't mean I'M not serious about playing soccer, because I AM. (*Very intense*) Last week, I stole the ball from the other team FOUR times, and scored FIVE goals on my own. They call me the Flying Phantom because I go so fast no one can see me. I just fly straight over the field and score. It's true, I'm the fastest runner we've got, just like my great-grand-pap. And as a reward after the game, my grandfather and dad always take me for pizza or ice-cream, or whatever I'm in the mood to eat. It doesn't matter if I win or lose either, because I'm rewarded for the WAY I play. Dad and grand-pap know I do my best no matter what. Actually, one of the best things about playing soccer is getting to spend time with my dad and pap after the games. Sometimes my brothers come along, too. It all depends if they're being nice to me that week.

Time: Approximately 1 minute 30 seconds

Age Range: 9+

VOCABULARY:

1. <u>centuries</u>- one century equals 100 years

2. <u>Brazil</u>- a country in South America
3. <u>legend</u>- an extremely famous or notorious person or story

Notes

_____
_____
_____
_____
_____
_____
_____
_____
_____
_____
_____
_____
_____
_____
_____
_____
_____
_____
_____
_____
_____
_____
_____
_____
_____
_____
_____
_____
_____
_____

CRUELTY
Female   Dramatic

It seems like people are so mean nowadays. No one takes the time to think they might hurt someone's feelings if they say something bad to them. I heard a boy yell out from a group of friends at a girl, and he called her "fat" and "ugly" to her face. She burst out in tears and they all LAUGHED at her. I couldn't believe it. I felt so bad for her. I wonder about the boys who made fun of her and what kind of family they must have to allow them to treat others so badly. Then there's another kind of cruelty. My older sister fights on the phone with her boyfriend all the time. She'll hang up on him, and tell me about how he tells her she is garbage and she's not pretty enough to be his girlfriend. Mind you, my sister is a model for several junior clothing lines. It's so sad but it's also pathetic that my sister doesn't stick up for herself and dump him. She lets him say whatever he wants. (PAUSE) Then there's the News. The News talks about terror, domestic violence, and hatred everywhere. But WHY? (BEAT) WHY do adults let kids get away with treating each other poorly? Teachers HEAR and SEE their students hurting each other with words, but more than half the teachers at my school don't do anything about it. My parents HEAR my sister fighting and crying with her boyfriend, but they still let her date a boy like that. It seems like no one wants to take the responsibility for correcting the wrong. People say, "It's not my business to mettle into other people's affairs". But when a building is bombed, or a little girl at school tries to kill herself … whose business is it then? OURS? The end result will always be based on what WE did or didn't do. It's time to make a difference … even when it's the hard thing to do. ESPECIALLY when it's the hard thing to do.

Time: Approximately 1 minute 45 seconds

Age Range: 9+

VOCABULARY:

1. <u>cruelty</u>- when a person causes pain to another person for the pleasure of hurting them

2. <u>pathetic</u>- here the term means "ridiculous"

3. <u>mettle</u>- to become involved with something

Notes

_____

_____

_____

_____

_____

_____

_____

_____

_____

_____

_____

_____

_____

_____

_____

_____

_____

_____

_____

_____

_____

_____

_____

_____

_____

_____

_____

_____

I LOVE YOU FOR ETERNITY
Anyone   Dramatic

....

When I was little, my mom and dad died from a plane accident. They were not in the plane, but they were working in one of the buildings that the plane hit. It was on the news at school, but I didn't understand what was happening. My Aunt Sue picked me up from class and told me mom and dad were lost in that building, and that firemen were going to find them. (BEAT) Even though I was really small, I knew when I saw the second plane hit the building that I'd never see mommy or daddy again. (PAUSE) I didn't cry because I was in shock. But I did cry much later. (PAUSE) I didn't eat for days, and it was months until I smiled again. I still have a little hole in my heart that won't ever be filled. When it is the anniversary of their death, and the deaths of thousands of people on that day, I always cry. My sadness will never pass. (BEAT) My Aunt Sue looks a lot like my mommy, and it helped me to feel better again for a while. But it isn't really the same. (BEAT) I'll always remember mommy and daddy tucking me into bed at night. We said our prayers and before they shut the door I'd say, "I love you for eternity". That means we love each other forever, no matter what. I still tell them that every night when Aunt Sue shuts my bedroom door. They are still with me, even though I can't see them, and I sometimes think I can hear them whisper back, "I love YOU for eternity".

Time: Approximately 1 minute 20 seconds

Age Range: 9+

VOCABULARY:

1. <u>shock</u>- a sudden upsetting or surprising event

2. <u>anniversary</u>- one day of the year that marks when something specific has occurred

3. <u>eternity</u>- forever

Notes

DON'T TOUCH THAT HAIR DYE
Female   Comedic

....

(Character wears a hat or scarf throughout monologue over her hair).

Oh! Ugh, mom? I really don't know how to tell you this so I'll just start from the beginning, okay? Because the beginning is a VERY good place to start. (BEAT) Once, Emily Hammerberger tried to start a story from the middle and it just didn't work out for her. (BEAT *listens to her mother*) I am NOT trying to avoid anything! Okay, okay. Well, when I came home from school today ... which I learned a LOT at school. Especially in English class. We started diagramming and did you know that – (BEAT, *listens to her mother again*) Anyway, right. The story. (*A meek giggle, then super fast pace in one or two breaths:*) I thought it'd be a really good idea if I tried to dye my hair by myself and I was having such a good time shaking the bottle and squirting it on my head that I started singing and dancing and tossing my head around like they do in hair dye commercials, and after that I had to wait for the dye to set and it took forever and after I rinsed it out I saw ... (*slowly*) I saw the wallpaper had little specs of hair dye all over it from me dancing with the dye in my hair. (*Closes eyes, expecting to get yelled at. This is a brief PAUSE. Slowly opens eyes*) Mom? Why are you smiling at me like that? Why aren't you screaming at me ferociously as I cower beneath you? (PAUSE) WHAT? I can't ... you can't really expect me to repaper the entire bathroom walls, can you? (BEAT) With my OWN money? (*VERY dramatic*) Oh, woe! Mother, darling, how can you be so CRUEL?! Oh woe is me! Never shall I dye my hair again. Never again! (*Falls melodramatically onto the floor.*)

Time: Approximately 1 minute 27 seconds

Age Range: 9+

VOCABULARY:

1. <u>avoid</u>- to keep away from something purposefully
2. <u>ferociously</u>- savagely violent and cruel
3. <u>cower</u>- to hide or take cover to avoid feeling ashamed
4. <u>melodrama</u>- over the top dramatic

Notes

COMPANY MEETING
Anyone   Comedic

••

(Taps on a microphone) Hello? Is this thing on? Testing, one, two, three. Alright, greaaaaat. How are you folks doing today? It's great to have you here. *(Points to someone in the audience)* Nice to see you again, Amy. *(Looks just above "Amy's" head)* Hey Phil, how are the kids? Great, great! *(Quickly)* Okay let's get down to business. I've called this meeting because our work environment needs a little something extra. We need a little ... SPICE in our work atmosphere. You know what I mean? *(Quickly, holds up hand in protest)* Before you answer that folks, I want you to know that I already came up with a solution. *(Very seriously)* We need sand-boxes. Sad-boxes, natural lighting, a smoothie machine, and palm trees. PLUS! We have three tanning beds on the way which will need installation. I thought maybe Phil could install those in the janitor supply room. (BEAT) Look folks, I'm sure this came as a shock, but I didn't expect so much negativity. If we can't move the office to Hawaii, like I proposed LAST week, then we need to bring Hawaii to US. (BEAT) What do you mean I MIGHT get fired for installing tanning beds? You can't fire a volunteer paper boy/girl. Not only is it a volunteer position, but no one else would WANT to work in this good-for-nothing, florescent-lit office! IT'S DEPRESSING! So let's bring the beds, and then we'll see WHO gets fired, OR pro-mo-ted!

Time: Approximately 1 minute 16 seconds

Age Range: 9+

VOCABULARY:

1. <u>environment</u>- the surroundings in which a person, plant, or animal lives OR operates

2. <u>atmosphere</u>- the tone or mood of a place

3. <u>solution</u>- the answer to a problem or question

4. <u>installation</u>- to set something up

Notes

COLD NIGHTS
Anyone   Dramatic

••

We live near the river. In the summer it's okay. The bridge is refreshing. But in the winter it's terrible. The wind feels like it could snap your nose off if you don't have something to cover it. But our home is strong enough to keep some of the wind out. (PAUSE) My brothers bring back new cardboard everyday to patch up the walls if an old piece gets too soggy. During the day it's nice because I go to school, and we're inside where there is heat and warm food. But when we go home, we're outside again. Under the bridge. The money dad gets from the city always goes to his drink fund. He says if he doesn't have his beer, he'll die, and then me and my brothers will be orphans! (PAUSE) I don't want that to happen. I don't tell my teachers at school that we lost our apartment, because then my brothers and I will be taken away from daddy and put into a group home. I know because my cousins were homeless once and they were split up and put into group homes until their mom could find an apartment. They told us stories which were NOT good. Group homes are scary places. (PAUSE) We'll get an apartment someday soon. I just don't know how soon.

Time: Approximately 1 minute 5 seconds

Age Range: 9+

VOCABULARY:

1. <u>refreshing</u>- pleasantly fresh; rejuvenating

2. <u>patch</u>- here, patch means a piece of material used for mending something

3. <u>orphans</u>- when both parents of a child pass away, the children are then referred to as orphans

Notes

WHO YOU ARE INSIDE
Anyone   Dramatic

I found a letter that a girl in my class wrote. It's really sad and I'm glad the bullies didn't find it before I did. They would make fun of her for writing it more than they already do. The girl's name is Samantha, and even though she's really, really nice, she doesn't have any friends. Kids make fun of her for being fa—(*stops before saying the word "fat"*) overweight. Her letter says she wishes she had a friend … ANYONE. She doesn't care if they're nice to her or not, as long as she has a place to sit during lunch and someone to talk to during recess. She wants someone to come to her house to visit on the weekends. The note is written to no one in particular. It was just lying on the floor in the hallway. I don't know who she was going to give it to. (PAUSE) The thing is, I know Sam. We've talked a lot of times, actually, when no one else could see me, and she is really a good person. Who cares if she is a little bigger than most of us? I'd rather be friends with someone who really cares about me than someone who just likes to have me around and fight all the time … like MOST of my friends do. (PAUSE) I don't know. Sometimes it's just hard to be friends with someone who is seen as a social outcast. I know the inside counts more than the outside, but it's hard to remember that when all your friends are looking at you weird for saying "hi" to the "loser" of the school. What should I do?

Time: Approximately 1 minute 16 seconds

Age Range: 9+

VOCABULARY:

1. <u>overweight</u>- when someone weighs more than is healthy for their age and size

2. <u>outcast</u>- someone who is not accepted into a social group

3. <u>weird</u>- strange

Notes

LET IT SNOW
Anyone   Comedic

··

I'm so exited! Tonight there is going to be a snowstorm, which means ... NO SCHOOL TOMORROW! My school calls days like tomorrow "Snow Days", because instead of going to school, kids go out and have fun in the snow. I already have my snow gear set out on my floor so that as soon as I wake up, I can throw it on and race out the door! I'm trying to decide what I should do fist. There are so many options! Dad tells me I'm "indecisive", like my mother. Ha! He says that like it's a BAD THING. But really, I don't know if I should build a snowman, make a snow angel, or just skip straight to the sledding. I like tubing, too. Tubing could prove to be the best option for what to do first, easily. (PAUSE) But then again, so could building a snowman. I'm going to have to sleep on it, I think. I know that no matter what, though, there will definitely be hot chocolate to drink when I come back into the house, which is almost as good as playing outside altogether! (*Stops speaking for a second while looking straight ahead, as if looking out a window*) It's already starting! I just LOVE snow days!

Time: Approximately 1 minute

Age Range: All Ages

VOCABULARY:

1. options- different things to choose from
2. indecisive- someone who has a hard time making a choice
3. decide- to make up your mind about a choice
4. tubing- (for snow) when you go down a snowy hill inside of an inner tube.

Notes

FULFF-BALL: THE INCREDIBLE CAT
Anyone   Comedic

···

(Fluff-Ball is lounging on a sofa at opening)

Hello, meow! I am Fluff-Ball, the world's most amazing cat ever. Meow can chase a ball up to 10 meows an hour. Ha! Get it, MEOWs an hour? Ha, ha. Anyway, I can play with string, chase a mouse, and jump onto the counter in a matter of seconds, simply to drink out of the cup that you were mew-sing over. Believe meow, though, (*stretches out over the sofa*) none of it is as easy as it looks. Suuuure I can tackle your leg with grace and valor when you LEAST expect it. But all that comes from strategic planning. There is serious business to consider when I want to get your undivided attention. I use what my owner calls, "reverse psychology", meow. Trust meow ... it WORKS. I use it to fake you out. Oh yeah! Just when you think meow is in the mood to be held, I jump out of your arms with a hiss, and hide under the sofa! Ha! Ahhhh. I love that one! So, (*rolls over*) the next time you think meow cats are just beautiful, lazy creatures ... think again. Because meows are SMART, too! Remember, it's all about the reverse psychology.

Time: Approximately 1 minute

Age Range: ALL AGES

VOCABULARY:

1. <u>musing</u>- (in this monologue it's spelled mew-sing for a play on words) Musing actually means to be absorbed in thought

2. <u>valor</u>- having a lot of courage in the face of danger

3. <u>undivided</u>- not separated, to be together, as one

4. <u>psychology</u>- scientific study of the human mind

Notes

_____
_____
_____
_____
_____
_____
_____
_____
_____
_____
_____
_____
_____
_____
_____
_____
_____
_____
_____
_____
_____
_____
_____
_____
_____
_____
_____
_____
_____
_____
_____
_____
_____
_____
_____

FOLLOW YOUR DREAMS
Male   Dramatic

••

Nothing can stop me from following my dreams. Not the way I look, not my height, not how much I weigh; nothing. If I want to be a basketball player and I'm a foot shorter than ALL the other guys, I will STILL try out for the team. And even if I'm not picked the first time, I'll KEEP trying out until I make it. If I'm poor and want to be the number one computer company president in the world, I'll figure out a way to do it. It doesn't matter how much money I have because I can work my way through college, and I will figure out a way to become the number one computer president in the world. No one can stop me. No one's words can stop me, no one's hands or fists will stop me. NOTHING will stop me from going after my dreams ... except myself. If I lose confidence, like a lot of people do, THEN I'll be defeated. But that is not going to happen because I will not LET it happen! Some of my friends, and even my family, are already saying I can't go after some of my dreams because it's "too hard for me". But I WILL go after my dreams, I already am! Some us dream great, some of us dream small, but the size of the dream doesn't matter. What matters is that you have a dream, and that you go after it.

Time: Approximately 1 minute

Age Range: ALL AGES

VOCABULARY:

1. <u>height-</u> the measurement of how tall a person or object may be

2. <u>weigh-</u> to measure (usually in pounds or kilos) how heavy someone or something may be

3. <u>confidence-</u> to feel 100% sure of yourself; you believe in yourself

4. <u>defeated-</u> to be beaten at something like a game or battle; to be on the losing side

Tested by kids!

Notes

_____

_____

_____

_____

_____

_____

_____

_____

_____

_____

_____

_____

_____

_____

_____

_____

_____

_____

_____

_____

_____

_____

_____

_____

_____

_____

_____

_____

_____

_____

_____

_____

_____

RULES ARE IMPORTANT
Anyone   Dramatic

....

My little brother didn't follow the rules, and because of THAT, he ended up in the emergency room. Mommy's rules for the house are simple. Number one: you can't throw balls or ANYTHING in the house. You always have to be outside when you want to throw something. We also can't wrestle in the house unless it is in the very middle of the game room, and that's the FINAL word! There are more rules than that, but for the sake of the story, we'll just continue. Well, Danny broke BOTH of those rules. He's really little; only two and a half! But he understands the rules already. Danny was in the kitchen wrestling with our puppy, Mrs. Wilson. I kept yelling, "Danny! You can't wrestle in the kitchen!" But he wouldn't listen, so I picked up Mrs. Wilson and put her in a locked room so Danny couldn't wrestle anymore. That made Danny mad, I guess, 'cause the next thing I see is an autographed baseball flying at my head, full-speed. I ducked, and the ball shattered a mirror that was directly over my head. I got out of the way luckily, but some glass flew so far that it hit Danny in the eye. He is okay now, thankfully, but he could have lost his eye-sight, or WORSE. Danny now knows about how important it is to follow the rules. But I was wrong too, because I should have told mommy or daddy about him wrestling with Mrs. Wilson FIRST, before I took her away and upset Danny enough to throw something at me.

Time: Approximately 1 minute 15 seconds

Age Range: ALL AGES

VOCABULARY:

1. simple- really easy
2. sake- for the purpose of doing something; to get something done

3. <u>autographed-</u> a person's signature, usually pertains to someone famous

4. <u>shattered-</u> to suddenly break something, and it falls into a lot of pieces

Notes

_____
_____
_____
_____
_____
_____
_____
_____
_____
_____
_____
_____
_____
_____
_____
_____
_____
_____
_____
_____
_____
_____
_____
_____
_____
_____
_____
_____
_____
_____
_____

READ, READ, READ
Female   Comedic

....

I HATE reading! It's all I ever do. My homework NEVER ends. The teacher tells me I need to, "Read <u>Charlotte's Web</u>, by Friday, and be ready for a quiz before the end of the day." She tells me this at 3:30PM on Thursday. How FAIR is that? Have you ever seen the SIZE of <u>Charlotte's Web</u>? It's not that I can't read that many pages in one night, because I definitely can. That's what I'm good at. They call me a prodigy child ... but just because I'm more brilliant than half the grown-ups I know, doesn't mean I don't want to go outside and play with other kids! (PAUSE) My grandmother made me do something totally morbid once. She had me write a thesis on the "Book of Job", and gave me one week to complete it, JUST so she could show me off to her card-playing friends. (BEAT) Read, read, read. Write, write, write. That's all anyone seems to think I'm good for; like I'm a little doll for their ENTERTAINMENT! Well, I'm NOT a doll! I'm a ___-year-old girl! And just because I'm a PRODIGY doesn't mean English work is ALL I like to do! Give me a break people. Let me act my age for one, and NOT my IQ!

Time: Approximately 1 minute

Age Range: ALL AGES

VOCABULARY:

1. <u>brilliant-</u> very, very smart

2. <u>thesis-</u> an essay written about a topic after the writer researches and studies the topic

3. <u>morbid-</u> abnormal and unhealthy interest in something odd; usually refers to death or disease, but this word is used here for comedic effect

Notes

I AM A NINJA!
Male   Comedic

••

(Slow and dramatic)

Behold! The ninja master of ALL ninja masters! It is I, Neo-spy. I have the greatest kung-fu moves in the world. No one … and I do mean no one … can defeat me. I taught myself all the moves I know. Like THIS! *(Kicks in the air)* And THIS! *(Karate chops the air)* And even (PAUSE) THIS. *(Spins, jumps, and kicks)* HOWEVER, you must not fear me. I am a fighter against evil, only. Not civilians. My real name can never be revealed, for I must protect my secret identity. But know THIS. If you ever need a protector, a REAL ninja fighter to guard your house, your car, your itty-bitty kitten … I am THERE. Just call Neo-spy! My swift ninja movements can protect anyone and any THING. Bad guys fear me, good guys want to BE me. *(Quick and perky)* Which can happen for you today if you purchase my, "Learn To Be ALMOST Like Me: The Greatest Ninja In The World Video Guide" now on DVD and Blu-ray. Yours today for just $24.99 plus shipping and handling. Call now, and you'll receive a free BONUS samurai sword at NO EXTRA COST! *(Back to slow and dramatic)* Don't make the mistake of being defenseless. Buy my DVD now, made by me, Neo-spy! This is one ninja who won't let you down. CALL NOW!

Time: Approximately 1 minute 10 seconds

Age Range: ALL AGES

VOCABULARY:

1. <u>behold-</u> to see or look at something

2. <u>defeat-</u> to be beaten at a battle or game; the losing side

3. <u>civilians-</u> people who are not involved with military or police … or in this case, ninjas

4. <u>purchase-</u> to buy something

Notes

SPIKY-KILLER
Male   Comedic

···

My pet poodle is the "best-est" dog in the whole wide world. I taught him really great tricks like fetching sticks, rolling over, and playing dead. I LOVE that one. But he has some cool tricks of his own. Spiky-Killer can open the lid on the toilet to get a drink. He can figure out which parts of the furniture are the easiest for ripping to shreds. Spiky-Killer can even bark so loud that my sister keeps away from my room! My poodle is like a personal body-guard, and he is also my best-friend. The reason my poodle's name is Spiky-Killer is because on his first trip to the dog groomers, the beautician accidentally cut him a Mohawk. He was such a cute little poodle that it was really funny to see him with spiky hair. Up until that point we were calling him Steve. But then after seeing him with the Mohawk, we started calling him Spiky-Killer. Then we went home and my mom dyed his hair purple. He looked really mean after that! Sorta.

Time: Approximately 1 minute

Age Range: ALL AGES

VOCABULARY:

1. <u>fetch-</u> when a dog runs to get and bring back something thrown into a short distance

2. <u>shred-</u> a strip of some material; or to rip material apart into pieces

3. <u>beautician-</u> a person's whose profession it is to make people (or animals) look nice

4. <u>Mohawk-</u> hairstyle inspired by Native Americans. The hair is shaved at the sides of the head, but a strip is left untouched in the middle to style pointing upward

Notes

GIVE ME A BREAK, I'M TWO!
Anyone   Comedic

••

Look mom, dad, this is really hard for me to tell you this, and I KNOW it's going to hurt you more than it hurts me but ... (*deep breath*) I'm getting tired of all the tutoring. I mean, first it was English, okay a kid's gotta learn English when they're living in America. But then came the Spanish, and the French, and the German. It was bad enough propping me up in front of those baby Socrates DVDs at age four months, but now I'm quad-lingual at the age of two! (PAUSE) And the algebraic formulas are getting dull as well. What's up with logarithms? I feel like my whole baby-hood is being taken away from me. (PAUSE) You know what I would really like to do BESIDES pull all of my books from the shelf and sit in the middle of them? I'd really like ... no ... I would be ECSTATIC if you two would jump up and down, clapping your hands frantically over me taking a poo on the pot, because that's NORMAL parental behavior! But since I was potty trained 15 months ago, the novelty has run out for you, I'm sure. Too late to get excited over little old me taking a poo-poo on the pot-pot! (PAUSE) Oh geeze, I didn't mean to shout, really I didn't. Look, all I'm asking is that you guys give me a break, you know? Toss me a bottle, give me a teddy bear, and let me run around screaming every now and then, and I'll be happy! I'm two years old for goodness sake, you gotta give me a break!

Time: Approximately 1 minute 25 seconds

Age Range: ALL AGES

VOCABULARY:

1. <u>tutoring-</u> to teach someone a subject outside of traditional classroom settings
2. <u>propping-</u> to lean on something for comfortable support

3. <u>algebraic-</u> involving algebra; algebra is a part of mathematics where letters and symbols are used to represent numbers

4. <u>ecstatic-</u> to be very, very excited

Notes

_____

_____

_____

_____

_____

_____

_____

_____

_____

_____

_____

_____

_____

_____

_____

_____

_____

_____

_____

_____

_____

_____

_____

_____

_____

_____

_____

_____

_____

_____

_____

_____

JEALOUSY
Female   Dramatic

••

(*Very melancholy:*) Sometimes I wish … I wish I could be HER. Elizabeth Martin. She is so perfect. (BEAT) Ever since elementary school she's had boyfriends, and they're ALWAYS the cutest in the class. She has perfect grades, and is a medal-winning gymnast. She's already being talked about for the Olympic qualifiers. (PAUSE) Her parents … (*thinks for a moment*) they have one of the nicest houses on THAT street. You know the street. The one where you aren't allowed to have a pool in your backyard UNLESS it's an in-ground pool? Think I'm kidding? I'm not. Seriously, how pretentious is THAT? But the point is THOSE people can afford it. (PAUSE) This is all materialistic, I do realize this, but these are not the only reasons I want to be Elizabeth Martin. She's the most popular girl in school. She is so sweet and nice to everyone … she makes me want to throw up. The star student, star athlete, star daughter, star GIRLFRIEND! It all makes me want to HATE this girl. She's too perfect! (PAUSE, *calming down*) They call this jealousy, don't they? Jealousy ruined a good number of people in our day. Like Cain, for instance. But I'm not going to KILL my cousin. I'm just tired of being in her shadow. (BEAT) It isn't easy being cousins with the most popular girl on earth.

Time: Approximately 1 minute 25 seconds

Age Range: 12

VOCABULARY:

1. <u>qualifiers-</u> when a person qualifies for something, they pass every test to permit them to move onto the next stage

2. <u>pretentious-</u> people who pretend to be very important, and think by showing off they can prove how "important" they are (They are more often than not rather Unimportant)

3. <u>materialistic-</u> people who think objects are very important and can bring happiness into their lives. For example, someone might care too much about what kind of car or cars they have, or being the most up-to-date in fashion, instead of concentrating on the real things that matter like friendship and family

Notes

WHAT NOW?
Male   Dramatic

....

(Moving to a New School)

I used to be the guy who picked on the new kid when they moved to our school. My group of five friends was ALL I cared about. No one new came into our crew, and no one old went out. We were a pack, and I was the leader. *(Laughs to himself, remembering the "good old days")* We used to make fun of the new kids SO bad! Even if there was nothing wrong with them, we'd just pick on them to mess with them a little. You know, harmless fun. Ha, ha! (PAUSE) Then the most horrible news imaginable came to my family. My dad got a job offer for engineering in another state. He TOOK the offer. We MOVED to another STATE, so my dad could make a few more dollars. I start my new school tomorrow. (BEAT) I'm terrified. There's going to be a group of guys who will torture me the way I tortured new kids, even though I'm perfectly normal. EXCEPT for the fact that now I'M the NEW GUY. (BEAT) So what now? What's next? Should I TRY to make new friends or just deal with the kids who will make fun of me? (BEAT) I kinda' wish now that I would have just let the new kids alone. But it's too late. Way too late.

Time: Approximately 1 minute 10 seconds

Age Range: 12

VOCABULARY:

1. <u>crew-</u> here, crew is slang for a group of friends
2. <u>harmless-</u> no harm; not causing harm or hurt
3. <u>engineering-</u> a career in science and technology that can involve machines and building
4. <u>offer-</u> presenting something that one can accept or decline

Notes

WHO DO I TELL?
Female   Dramatic

••

I'm really scared for my friend, Trish. She is getting too skinny. We are both the same height, but Trish weighs 25 pounds less than me. She thinks she looks fat. I say things to her like, "If you think YOU'RE fat, I don't want to know what I look like!" It's just a joke to make her realize she is not fat at all. But she doesn't get it. (BEAT) I don't know what to do, I feel like I need to help her in some way, but don't know how. She refuses to eat lunch. Trish freaks out if she eats a cracker, and then she runs a mile to burn off the calories. (PAUSE) You know, Trish's mom really cares about her. But she is never home when Trish is … her mom is a bartender so just as Trish is getting home from school, her mom is leaving for work. Trish bragged to me that when she and her mom actually DO get to see each other, Trish will make up some excuse to go do homework, or go for a run. They never get to talk, and I KNOW her mother hasn't seen her wearing non-baggy clothing. (BEAT) The baggy clothes cover up how skinny Trish really is. She looks disgusting … like a walking skeleton. I got so upset yesterday that … I actually TOLD her she looked liked Death walking. (BEAT) I didn't mean to make her cry. I didn't mean to cry, either. We fought for a half hour after I said that to her. She swore she is never going to talk to me again, and that I'm just jealous of how she looks. But it isn't true! (BEAT) Tomorrow I'm going to the school counselor. Someone needs to help her, since I obviously can't. I'm so afraid to lose my best friend … forever.

Time: Approximately 1 minute 30 seconds

Age Range: 11+

VOCABULARY:

1. <u>refuse-</u> to not accept something (like the truth, or an object)

2. <u>obviously-</u> easily understood; clear

3. <u>counselor-</u> someone whose profession it is to listen to another person's problems and help them out

Notes

_____
_____
_____
_____
_____
_____
_____
_____
_____
_____
_____
_____
_____
_____
_____
_____
_____
_____
_____
_____
_____
_____
_____
_____
_____
_____
_____
_____
_____
_____
_____
_____
_____
_____
_____
_____

I NEED BRACES
Male   Dramatic

••

I need braces for my teeth very badly. I have bucked teeth and some are missing which makes my teeth really crooked. My parents tell me that braces are too expensive and that my teeth will straighten out on their own. But HOW? I get made fun of so much for the way my teeth are. I'd pay a million dollars just for THAT to stop. Look, I don't want your pity, so please don't think I'm asking for it. I just want to know HOW I can convince my parents to get me braces. Girls think I'm cute until I smile at them. Then they scream and run the other way. I didn't realize how bad it was until an old woman saw me two years ago and said, "Oh! What a cute litt-" ... the word "little" stopped when I opened my mouth, and she barely managed to stammer out, "Oh! I thought you were someone else." SHE wasn't the prettiest old lady I ever saw either, but she made sure I KNEW I was ugly just because of my darned-picket-fenced teeth! I've talked about this problem with the school counselor, but there's nothing anyone can do for me EXCEPT my parents. (*Deep breath, on the first* **word** *sigh out:*) I guess all I can do is keep working the paper route so I can eventually buy braces myself!

Time: Approximately 1 minute 5 seconds

Age Range: 11+

VOCABULARY:

1. <u>crooked-</u> when something that is supposed to be straight or orderly, is not

2. <u>convince-</u> to make someone totally and completely believe in something you tell them

3. <u>stammer-</u> to stumble over your words; barely get a sentence out

Notes

CAUGHT
Male   Dramatic

••

I was at the mall yesterday with my best friend, Ken. We were checking out some video games and things when suddenly I saw this girl I really like. Her name is Jerica. This girl, you gotta understand, is the most beautiful thing I've ever seen. Long red hair, and dark green eyes. She looks like a model. Well, Jerica saw us and came over to talk. We three were chatting for a bit, and then Jerica happens to mention this purse she REALLY likes, you know? She wanted this purse So bad. So Ken pulls me aside and says, "Hey man, you really like this chick, right?" I say, "Yeah, dude, right." He says, "Go get her the purse, then." I didn't have any cash on me, and I didn't know what else to do. I wanted to impress Jerica by getting her that purse; I HAD to get that bag one way or another. So ... I stole it. I grabbed it, snapped the security tag off, and walked right out of the store. I was about two feet out the door when a hand grabbed my shoulder. It was a security guard. (PAUSE) I've never been in so much trouble in my life. Jerica doesn't even look at me in class now. I think she's embarrassed that I wanted to impress her so much that I stole the bag. It was stupid, I know. Not only did I NOT impress Jerica, but I was grounded for over a month, and Ken isn't allowed to hang out with me anymore. I'm NEVER doing anything that idiotic and illegal ever again.

Time: Approximately 1 minute 15 seconds

Age Range: 11+

VOCABULARY:

1. impress- to make someone think very highly of you
2. embarrassed- when a person feels ashamed for something they did
3. idiotic- a stupid action

Notes

COLOR DOESN'T MATTER
Anyone   Dramatic

My ex-best friend's dad makes me really angry. He is mean to people who are a different color than he is. When Ben and I went to school together, we were in a private elementary school with an all-white student body. The first African American student came to school when we were in fourth grade. HE got along with everyone. His grades were good, and he was a lot of fun to play with in sports. He's actually one of my best friends, now. But Ben's dad didn't like that our new classmate was another color other than white. When he found out that Ben and I were hanging out with him and becoming good friends, he screamed at Ben for three hours, non-stop. Someone actually called the police because of the yelling, and the offensive things he was shouting. The police came and told Mr. Parker that he had to keep it down, and that he was a disruption to the neighborhood. Mr. Parker yelled back: "I'll tell YOU what's a disruption to the neighborhood! Those BLACK people moving into it!" (BEAT) When the officer told him to settle down, Mr. Parker took a swing at the officer's head, missed, and fell over. I guess he was drunk like he usually is. (PAUSE) Ben moved away after that and goes to another school now. I saw him at a baseball game by sheer chance. He smiled and said, "hi", but that was all. It stinks that we can't be friends anymore. Mom says she doesn't want me to be around violent and prejudiced adults. (BEAT) Skin color just doesn't matter. I WISH Mr. Parker could see that.

Time: Approximately 1 minute 20 seconds

Age Range: 10+

VOCABULARY:

1. <u>student body-</u> the population of students at a school

2. <u>disruption-</u> to take attention away from something, usually in a rude manner

3. <u>sheer-</u> here, sheer means "only by chance"

4. <u>prejudiced-</u> a hateful opinion (that is **not** based on facts) about another person or another culture's differences to your own

Notes

_____

_____

_____

_____

_____

_____

_____

_____

_____

_____

_____

_____

_____

_____

_____

_____

_____

_____

_____

_____

_____

_____

_____

_____

_____

I'M PRETTY, TOO
Female   Dramatic

··

There is a boy in my class, Michael, who I have liked for three years. He's really cute and has big brown eyes, and the prettiest black hair. (PAUSE) I don't think he likes me, though. I wrote him a letter last week to tell him I admired him, just to see what he'd say. A whole day went by, and he didn't say anything back. I thought maybe there was a chance that he might like me, too. But then … the next day a really pretty girl in my class, Crystal, came over to me and handed me the letter back, with x's all over it. (PAUSE, *sadly:*) Michael showed EVERYBODY my letter. One of his guy friends came up to me and said, "He doesn't like you. He doesn't even know you. Besides, you aren't pretty enough. He likes Crystal, anyway." (BEAT) I cried for the rest of the day. But just because Michael likes Crystal doesn't mean that he can't like me. Crystal is pretty, but I'm pretty, too! I have beautiful (*insert color of actor's eyes here*) eyes, and I am MUCH friendlier than Crystal. It's not fair for someone to say I'm not pretty enough. I AM VERY PRETTY! (PAUSE) It just … it was cruel of Michael's friend to say what he said to me! He was ugly, anyway. He's just mad because no one likes HIM. (BEAT) Maybe he's right. Maybe I am just an ugly, stupid cow. Michael deserves Crystal anyway.

Time: Approximately 1 minute 25 seconds

Age Range: 11+

VOCABULARY:

1. <u>admire-</u> to like or appreciate someone or something very much

2. <u>cruel-</u> to cause pain or suffering

3. <u>deserves-</u> to do something that you're worthy of (good or bad)

Notes

_____
_____
_____
_____
_____
_____
_____
_____
_____
_____
_____
_____
_____
_____
_____
_____
_____
_____
_____
_____
_____
_____
_____
_____
_____
_____
_____
_____
_____
_____
_____
_____
_____
_____
_____
_____

YOU NEVER KNOW
Male   Dramatic

....

It bothers me when people judge others without even knowing them. There is a kid who sits on the street corner next to my school every morning before classes start. He just sits there. No matter how cold or hot. When school begins he always comes inside 10 minutes late and gets detention everyday for being tardy. He LIKES to get detention. He'll disrupt class, and he is sent to the principal's office at LEAST twice a week. Everyone in my grade always talks about him and about how bad he is. But one day I overheard the teachers saying how in after-school detention he is an ANGEL; a totally different person. He helps them clean up the room and reads, and does his homework. I would never imagine that HE would actually be NICE and GOOD like that. Mom told me not to judge other people because you never know about their personal lives or past experiences. I didn't know what she meant at first. Then I saw the boy and his dad at the supermarket and I knew what she meant right away. His dad yelled at him to grab something off the shelf, but then said, "Not THAT, stupid, the OTHER one." Then he hit the side of the boy's head. I felt so bad. He gets to school early and makes sure to stay late because he doesn't want to be at home. He's mean to everyone, because that's how HE has always been treated. (PAUSE) Please don't judge people too harshly or too quickly. Even if you think you know them ... 'cause chances are, you really don't.

Time: Approximately 1 minute 15 seconds

Age Range: 10+

VOCABULARY:

1. judge- to make a decision about someone before you get to know them

2.   <u>disrupt-</u> to interrupt something like when a teacher is speaking to the class and someone talks without raising their hand

3. <u>appearances-</u> that way that someone looks on the outside

4. <u>harsh-</u> cruel or severe

Notes

_____

_____

_____

_____

_____

_____

_____

_____

_____

_____

_____

_____

_____

_____

_____

_____

_____

_____

_____

_____

_____

_____

_____

_____

_____

_____

_____

STAY AWAY FROM ALCOHOL
Anyone   Dramatic

···

My older brother Jesse is really bad. He listens to music really loud and it drives our neighbors crazy. They're always calling our house to yell at my brother, or at my parents for letting him listen to, "that obnoxious, no-good music". My parents just shrug their shoulders and say, "Well, he's a teenage boy, what do you expect?" But it's more than that, and it makes me mad because my parents refuse to see the real problem. Jesse is always shutting his door and smoking out his window. I told on him once and my parents searched his room, but didn't find any tobacco. My brother tried to beat me up after that for telling, but I ran as fast as I could to get away. He also drinks alcohol with his friends on the weekends. Jesse isn't old enough to drink alcohol, OR smoke cigarettes. (*Slowly, to make a point:*) He's fifteen and thinks he's twenty-one. His grades are getting worse and worse and all my parents can say is that he's just being a kid. Yeah, a really OFF-TRACK kid! Last weekend the police busted a party where the kids were drinking alcohol under the age of twenty-one, and GUESS WHO was there? Jesse was drunk and tried to get away from the police by jumping out of a second-story window. He ended up breaking his left leg and arm, and got citations for under-age drinking. It came as a shock to my parents. I have no idea WHY since they knew about his behavior, but now they REALLY know, I guess. It just goes to show that until you're twenty-one and older, you should stay away from alcohol, and stay on-track.

Time: Approximately 1 minute 20 seconds

Age Range: 10+

VOCABULARY:

1. <u>obnoxious-</u> extremely unpleasant behavior, and it draws attention to the person for negative reasons

2. refuse- to show that someone is not willing to do or acknowledge something

3. citations- a fine that the police give to people who disobey the law

Notes

_____
_____
_____
_____
_____
_____
_____
_____
_____
_____
_____
_____
_____
_____
_____
_____
_____
_____
_____
_____
_____
_____
_____
_____
_____
_____
_____
_____
_____
_____
_____

PREJUDICE AGAINST ANOTHER RELIGION
Anyone   Dramatic

The people that live on my street are what my mother calls PREJUDICED. She says that is an ugly word for ugly people. The folks on my street are not literally ugly, but some are on the INSIDE. Once I had a friend over who is another religion other than me. They have to wear their hair and clothes a different way, but I never thought much about it! We were outside on our bikes when the neighbors yelled something VERY inappropriate to us. When I asked my mom what it meant, she said she was "so sorry" to my friend, and made a phone call to the house that yelled at us. She argued for 20 minutes at our neighbors. When dad got home he took my friend back to their house, and on the way home, I told him what had happened. My friend hasn't been allowed to come back over, not because MY parents don't allow them, but because THEIR parents don't allow it. (PAUSE) Dad hates when mom, (*mocking dad's voice*) "makes it her business to tell people what to think". But if she didn't stand up for us, who would have? (*Gets a little angry*) Just because my friend is a different religion than me and the people on my street, and has to wear special clothes, doesn't mean they're bad, or mean, or stupid! It doesn't mean ANY of those things! I'm glad my mom said something to the neighbors. People think they can say whatever they want to whomever they want. Prejudice is so hateful ... sometimes I wish we could just move away from our street to a place where people aren't so horrible, and where they CAN accept the differences of others.

Time: Approximately 1 minute 20 seconds

Age Range: 10+

VOCABULARY:

1. <u>prejudice-</u> a hateful opinion (that is **not** based on facts) about another person or another culture's differences to your own

2. <u>inappropriate-</u> behavior that is completely unacceptable for **anybody**

3. <u>accept-</u> to welcome someone for who they are, no matter what is different about them; being respectful of another person's differences

Notes

_____
_____
_____
_____
_____
_____
_____
_____
_____
_____
_____
_____
_____
_____
_____
_____
_____
_____
_____
_____
_____
_____
_____
_____
_____

I'M A LONER
Female   Dramatic

··

I sit at the lunch table by myself. Well, there are other people around me, but they just kinda' roll their eyes at me. (BEAT) The cute boys always talk to the popular girls ... not to a loner like me. Those girls are very pretty, some of them are cheerleaders. I tried out for the cheer team ... but I didn't make it. (BEAT) The most popular boy and the most popular girl are actually going together right now. He plays soccer and she cheers for his team. They make a good couple. (BEAT) My mom says that I shouldn't worry about boys right now because I'm too young, and that I'll be sure to have a boyfriend in high school because I AM pretty. (PAUSE) But the boys at my school must not think I'm attractive because no one wants to be MY boyfriend, let alone talk to me. I'm a loser anyway. I can't seem to get anything right. I don't have friends. I'm picked last in gym class. I get C's and D's on my tests. And I have to deal with people on the bus ride home. I'd rather be thrown down a well than have to go home on the bus with those jerks again. The kids on the bus are so mean to me. I wish they'd just leave me alone. So what if I'm a loner? It doesn't mean I deserve to be miserable.

Time: Approximately 1 minute 15 seconds

Age Range: 12

VOCABULARY:

1. <u>attractive-</u> a way of saying good-looking
2. <u>well-</u> a hole in the ground that holds fresh water
3. <u>miserable-</u> completely unhappy; wretched

Notes

THE ACCIDENT
Anyone   Dramatic

....

Accidents happen. Sometimes they're small, little mistakes, and other times ... (PAUSE) I was on a camping trip with my family. My sister Haley, she has always been the adventurous one, was so excited about this trip. It's all she could talk about for weeks. She would say, "I'm going to go rock climbing, and white water rafting, and I'm going to make s'mores every night, and eat so many I'll explode!" Even though she was into extreme, outdoorsy activities, she was always very safe with her actions. But accidents can happen even when you're very careful. (BEAT) We were swimming one afternoon on the trip, and were jumping off a rock into the water. Our parents told us not to dive, because we were not sure how deep the water was. Diving into shallow water can be very harmful, if not fatal. Well, after a few jumps my sister decided to dive in, because her feet never touched the bottom, and she figured the water was probably deep enough for diving. She dove in, but after several seconds, Haley still didn't emerge. I thought she was playing a bad joke. It's NOT funny to stay under water and make your family worry about you. (PAUSE) But then her body bobbed up onto the water's surface. My dad jumped in and pulled her out of the water. She wasn't breathing. Dad gave her CPR, while my mom dialed 9-1-1. Haley coughed up some water and started to breathe, but she wasn't awake. (BEAT) A helicopter came and took Haley to the nearest hospital, 50 miles away. She was in a coma for three weeks. When she awoke, Haley was told she had suffered a spinal injury and would never be able to walk again, and possibly never have control of her arms. My adventurous little sister had learned a life-altering lesson about the importance of safety and caution ... a little too late. Even when you think something is safe, accidents can still happen.

Time: Approximately 1 minute 53 seconds

Age Range: 11+

VOCABULARY:

1. fatal- to cause death

2. CPR- the abbreviation for cardiopulmonary resuscitation, which is an emergency medical procedure for restoring normal heartbeat and breathing

3. spinal- relating to the spine, which extends from your skull to the small of your back

4. caution- when a person is careful to avoid danger or mistakes

Notes

I AM PRINCE PUMPERNICKELSLACKER (PUMPER-NICKEL-SLACKER)
Male   Comedic

···

*(British accent recommended. Actor
has a picture of a duck).*

Hello, I am Prince Pumpernickelslacker! My companion, this duck, is Mr. McQuacker. I live in a palace upon yonder hill, where there is plenty of time for me to kill. The year is 1815 and my father is king. He has chopped off some heads, and that sort of thing. I have tea with my mother 'most everyday, while Mr. McQuacker swims in the bay. Upon dad's return we set out to hunt, and shoot a goose or two, but ne'er the runts. You stare at me strangely, 'cause I like my game, but shooting in these days held zero shame. If I had a choice, I'd ne'er shoot a gun, but what else is there to do in these days for fun? 1815 was a rather bland year, that is, 'til some excitement came up 'round here! I speak of the great battle at Waterloo, when we beat Napoleon 20 to 2. Okay, so I don't really know the numbers to tell, but we still beat them, yes, we gave them ... heck. My family name Pumpernickleslacker, had reigned for years until Mr. McQuacker had some small trouble with my father one winter. Dad wanted duck for Christmas dinner. Christmas morning dad set out to hunt, and upon his return came in with a bunt. The bunt was from aunty who lives down the hill, but in his other hand was a duck's bill. I cried, and I screamed, and I hollered out TREASON! Our downfall of reign was for this very reason. The country mistook my shouting for fact, and so we fled to France, to ne'er look back. This is my story whether true or fable, I dictated the account as best as I'm able. Thank you for listening intensely to me, as for myself, I am off to drink tea.

Time: Approximately 1 minute 20 seconds

Age Range: 10+

Suggested for staged reading.

VOCABULARY:

5. <u>yonder-</u> a way of saying "beyond"

6. <u>reigned-</u> to rule a kingdom

7. <u>bunt-</u> a type of cake

8. <u>ne'er-</u> an abbreviated way of saying "never", used commonly in ancient poetry

Notes

_____

_____

_____

_____

_____

_____

_____

_____

_____

_____

_____

_____

_____

_____

_____

_____

_____

_____

_____

_____

_____

_____

_____

34834726R00123

Made in the USA
San Bernardino, CA
08 June 2016